Science, Grade 2

Table of Contents

Unit 3: Life Science

Introduction

Children see the world around them and ask questions that naturally lead into the lessons that they will be taught in science. Science is exciting to children because it answers their questions about themselves and the world around them—their immediate world and their larger environment. They should be encouraged to observe their world, the things in it, and how things interact. A basic understanding of science boosts students' understanding of the world around them.

Organization

Science provides information on a variety of basic science concepts. It is broken into three units: Physical Science, Earth and Space Science, and Life Science. Each unit contains concise background information on the unit's topics, as well as exercises and activities to reinforce students' knowledge and understanding of basic principles of science and the world around them.

This book contains three types of pages:
- Concise background information is provided for each unit. These pages are intended for the teacher's use or for helpers to read to the class.

- Assessments are included for use as tests or practice for the students. These pages are meant to be reproduced.

- Activity pages contain information on a subject, or they list the materials and steps necessary for students to complete a project. Questions for students to answer are also included on these pages as a type of performance assessment. As much as possible, these activities include most of the multiple intelligences so students can use their strengths to achieve a well-balanced learning style. These pages are also meant for reproduction for use by students.

Use

Science is designed for independent use by students who have been introduced to the skills and concepts described. Copies of the activities can be given to individuals, pairs of students, or small groups for completion. They may also be used as a center activity. If students are familiar with the content, the worksheets may also be used as homework.

Hands-On Experience

An understanding of science is best promoted by hands-on experience. *Science* provides a wide variety of classroom activities for students to do. But students also need real-life exposure to their world. Playgrounds, parks, and vacant lots are handy study sites to observe many of nature's forces and changes.

It is essential that students be given sufficient concrete examples of scientific concepts. Appropriate manipulatives can be bought or made from common everyday objects. Most of the activity pages can be completed with materials easily accessible to the students.

Suggestions for Use
- **Bulletin Board:** Display completed work to show student progress.

- **Portfolios:** Have your students maintain a portfolio of their completed exercises and activities or of newspaper articles about current events in science. This portfolio can help you in performance assessment.

- **Assessments:** Use the overall and unit assessments as diagnostic tools by administering them before students begin the activities. After students have completed each unit, let them retake the unit test to see the progress they have made.

- **Center Activities:** Use the worksheets as a center activity to give students the opportunity to work cooperatively.

- **Fun:** Have fun with these activities while you and your students uncover the basic principles of science.

FOSS Correlation

The Full Option Science System™ (FOSS) was developed at the University of California at Berkeley. It is a coordinated science curriculum organized into four categories: Life Science; Physical Science; Earth Science; and Scientific Reasoning and Technology. Under each category are various modules that span two grade levels. The modules for this grade level are highlighted below.

Physical Science
- Solids and Liquids: 15, 16, 18, 21, 23, 25, 26, 29, 56
- Balance and Motion: 30–42

Earth Science
- Air and Weather: 87, 91, 93–104
- Pebbles, Sand, and Silt: 73–76, 78, 80–84

Life Science
- Insects: 158–159
- New Plants: 132–147

Overall Assessment

Use a word from the box to complete each sentence.

see	soft	heavy	straight
liquid	throats	force	Sun

1. Water is a _____.

2. A _____ is a push or a pull.

3. A strong force is needed to move _____ things.

4. You need light to _____ things.

5. We get most of our light from the _____.

6. Light moves in a _____ line.

7. A whisper is a _____ sound.

8. People make sounds with their _____.

GO ON TO THE NEXT PAGE ☞

Overall Assessment, p. 2

☐ **Read each sentence. Circle _true_ or _false_.**

9. Soil is made of many things.   true   false

10. Moving air is called snow.   true   false

11. Nine planets orbit around the Sun.   true   false

12. Earth gets light and heat from the Sun.   true   false

☐ **Darken the letter of the answer that best completes the sentence.**

13. Most of the Earth is covered by _____.
    Ⓐ grass
    Ⓑ woods
    Ⓒ water

14. Land is made of soil and _____.
    Ⓐ rock
    Ⓑ Sun
    Ⓒ wind

15. Rain comes from _____.
    Ⓐ erosion
    Ⓑ clouds
    Ⓒ degrees

16. The _____ revolves around the Earth.
    Ⓐ Sun
    Ⓑ Moon
    Ⓒ star

GO ON TO THE NEXT PAGE ☞

Overall Assessment, p. 3

 Use a word from the box to complete each sentence.

safe	Seeds	roots	bicycle
mammals	habitat	soil	leaves

17. The natural home of a plant or an animal is called a

_____.

18. The _____ of a plant hold it in the ground.

19. The _____ make food for the plant.

20. _____ grow into new plants.

21. Roots get water from the _____.

22. Humans and whales are _____.

23. It is not _____ to play in the street.

24. Use correct hand signals when riding your

_____.

Unit 1: Physical Science

BACKGROUND INFORMATION

Matter

Matter is all around. It is everything that we see and touch. Matter has mass, or weight, and takes up space. Matter is identified in three forms: solid, liquid, and gas. Matter can be easily described by its properties, both physical and chemical. Physical properties describe how a substance looks, which includes color, shape, texture, melting point, and boiling point. Chemical properties tell how something reacts with another substance so that it changes in its appearance, taste, or smell. For example, iron reacts with oxygen and water to make a new substance, rust.

All matter is made up of tiny particles called molecules. Molecules are made up of even smaller particles called atoms. Molecules cannot be seen with a microscope, but students can understand a substance's properties by using their senses when performing simple experiments. For example, if sugar is dissolved in water, the sugar cannot be seen; but it can be detected through taste because the water is sweet.

Solids, Liquids, and Gases

The state of matter is determined by the density of the molecules and how fast they move. In a solid, the molecules are attracted to each other and are tightly held together. The movement of the particles is limited; they vibrate only. Therefore, a solid has a definite shape and volume. A solid's mass is measured in grams (g), a metric weight that is a scientific measurement standard.

Liquids have a definite volume, but they take the shape of the container. The molecules in a liquid are not packed as tightly, so they can move about more freely and easily by sliding over each other. This movement is what makes a liquid take the shape of the container. The volume of a liquid is measured in milliliters (mL), the scientific standard measurement for liquid.

Gas is the third state of matter. In a gas, the molecules are far apart and move very quickly and randomly in all directions. They bounce off each other when they collide. Gas has no definite shape or volume. Gas, therefore, expands to take the shape of a container. Gas is measured in milliliters (mL).

Changes in Matter

All matter can change form, meaning it can change from one state to another. When matter changes, nothing is lost or gained; the molecules stay the same. The addition or the removal of heat causes the molecules to get closer or farther apart. The greater the amount of heat, the faster the molecules move. These changes in the density and the speed of a substance's molecules cause the state of matter to change.

When a solid is heated, the molecules expand. They vibrate faster and slip out of position, resulting in the solid changing into a liquid. This process is called melting, and the point at which the solid changes to a liquid is called the melting point. All matter, including rocks, has a melting point. The most commonly recognized melting point (or freezing point) is that of water, which is 0° on the Celsius scale or 32° on the Fahrenheit scale. Even with this change, the structure of the molecules stays the same.

When liquid is heated, the loose molecules continue to expand. The vibration increases, causing them to collide with each other and move in all directions. When the boiling point is reached, the liquid changes into a gas. The most commonly recognized boiling point is that of water. It boils at 100° Celsius or 212° Fahrenheit. This process is called evaporation. Again, the molecules stay the same; nothing is lost or gained when the matter changes states.

The removal of heat causes the reverse changes in matter. Through condensation, a gas is cooled, and the molecules contract. They stop colliding and return to their loose state, thus becoming a liquid. If heat is removed to the point that a liquid reaches its freezing point, a liquid will become a solid. The molecules are densely packed and cannot slide around. In any of these changes, nothing is lost or gained; only the properties of matter change.

Physical Changes

Matter can be changed in two ways, either in a physical change or in a chemical change. A physical change in matter is a change in which the molecules of a substance or substances do not change. There are three kinds of physical change. When matter changes states, as explained above, it is one kind of physical change. A second kind of physical change takes place when a mixture is made. A mixture is a combination of substances in which the molecules of the substances diffuse evenly. Each substance retains its own properties and can be detected by the senses. A third kind of physical change takes place when the shape of a substance is changed through cutting, ripping, or grinding. A log can be cut into many pieces. What remains are sawdust and cut logs. The molecules of the log itself have not changed.

Chemical Changes

When the molecules of a substance change, a chemical change has taken place. A new substance is always made in a chemical change, but molecules are never lost. Even though new molecules are made, the same number of atoms exists. Energy, generally in the form of heat, causes the atoms in molecules to form different molecules. Baking is a common example of chemical change. Chemical changes also occur in the human body. Through chemical changes, food and oxygen react in the body's cells to create energy to make the body work.

Force

A force is simply a push or a pull. Forces can be balanced or unbalanced, and the interactions of these kind of forces create motion. If forces are balanced, there is no movement. Forces also differ in size and direction. To move a book, it takes a small amount of force; but to move a bookshelf, it would take much more force. Forces can come from up, down, left, and right.

A force can be measured. Force is measured in newtons. Forces can be added and subtracted. If forces are going in the same direction, they are added. For example, if someone is pushing a wagon and another person is pulling the wagon, the amount of forces being exerted can be added together. However, if people are pulling in opposite directions, as in a tug-of-war, the forces would be subtracted. The team having the greater number of newtons would have a greater force and would win.

Gravity

Gravity is a force that attracts all objects that have mass. It is the force that keeps all objects from flying off the surface of the Earth. It is also the force that keeps the planets, Moon, and stars in orbit. Everything on Earth is pulled to the center of the Earth by this unseen force. Sir Isaac Newton called this force gravitation. The more massive an object, the greater the gravitational force that will be exerted. On Earth, the force of gravitation is about 9.8 newtons per kilometer.

A concept that is difficult for students to understand is the difference in the terms *mass* and *weight*. Mass is the measure of the amount of matter in an object. Mass is measured in grams (g). Weight is the measure of the force of gravity on an object. A spring scale measures weight using newtons. When students step on a scale, they are actually measuring their mass, since weight is measured in newtons. It can best be explained by comparing the mass and weight of a person on Earth and on the Moon. The mass of the person stays the same in either place. However, the weight of the person on the Moon will be one sixth of the weight on Earth. The gravitational pull is one sixth less on the Moon since the Moon has less mass.

Motion

The motion of an object is the result when a variety of forces interact. A change in motion occurs if a still object moves, or an object already in motion changes speed or direction. Two different forces, acting in opposite directions, will interact so an object will not move. These forces are considered balanced forces. An unbalanced force results when a force is placed on an object either at rest or in motion, making the object change its state. The object will move faster as the forces become more unbalanced. Suppose a soccer ball is on the field. It is in a state of rest; the forces are balanced. But if someone kicks the ball, the force of the kick makes the ball move. The greater the force, the faster the ball will go, and the farther it will go.

Friction

Friction is a force that keeps resting objects from moving and tends to slow motion when one object rubs against another object. Every motion is affected by friction. An object's surface determines the amount of friction. Rough surfaces create more friction. Smooth surfaces have less friction, so motion is easier. Mass and surface areas of objects also affect the amount of friction. The heavier an object is, the greater the amount of friction. Similarly, when large surface areas come into contact during motion, friction is greater. By reducing the contact of the surface areas, such as by using wheels, the object can be moved more easily. In some cases, friction can be reduced by using lubricants, materials like oil or soap. Lubricants coat the surface of an object to decrease rubbing.

Light

Light is another form of energy given off in tiny particles called photons. Photons are not a kind of matter, but they move in waves. Thus, light energy exhibits characteristics of both particles and waves.

Like sound waves, light waves can move through all matter. However, whereas sound cannot move through a vacuum, photons can. Photons move quickly, too, more quickly than anything else in nature. They travel at a rate of about 300,000 kilometers per second through air, whereas sound only travels 334 meters per second.

Light can be produced from both natural and artificial sources. Natural light is produced by the Sun, the most important source, stars, and fireflies. Light from a natural source is called white light. Artificial light is the product of electricity and reactions that can be controlled, such as flashlights, light bulbs, fires, and candles. Some objects appear to be a light source, but they simply reflect a natural light source. The Moon is an example of a reflective object. Light from the Sun strikes the Moon. The light bounces back or reflects, making the Moon look as if it is emitting a light.

Movement of Light

Light travels in a straight path from its source, moving away in all directions. But the farther a light beam is from its source, the more the beams diffuse. Light near its source is brighter and more intense because the photons are more dense. Conversely, the farther you move away from the light source, the dimmer the light appears. Because light has the tendency to move in a straight line, we cannot see around corners.

When light hits an object, the object blocks the light, causing a shadow to form. A shadow is the dark area behind an object resulting from the blocking of light waves. Shadows are made when the object is in the path of a light beam. Moreover, the closer the object is to the source, the sharper the shadow will be. The farther an object is from the light source, the more the shadow will be blurred around the edges.

The makeup of the object affects the movement of the light beam. Materials are identified as either transparent, translucent, or opaque. A transparent object, like glass and clear plastic, allows the light to move through, much like a sound wave moves through a solid. Light essentially travels in a straight path through a transparent object. Transparent objects are clear and easily seen through. A translucent object is blurry when you look through it. As light travels through a translucent object, it bends slightly. Because the light bends, the material looks blurry. Opaque objects totally block the light. Since light cannot travel through an opaque object, you cannot see through it.

Reflection and Absorption

Most objects do not produce light. We can see them because of reflection and absorption. Reflection occurs when a light beam collides with an object. The beam bounces back, much like a ball thrown against the floor. When the reflected light hits the eye, we can see the object. Absorption is the process in which a light beam, or parts of a light beam, soak into the object. Some objects absorb part of the beam, while the rest of the beam is reflected.

Flat Reflectors

The surface of an object also affects the reaction of light. Some surfaces are shiny and smooth. Light reflects, or bounces off, easily. Mirrors and polished metals are good reflectors. When a light beam collides with a flat reflective surface, the beam bounces back at a corresponding angle. The incoming beam creates the angle of incidence, which is equal to the angle of reflection, created by the outgoing beam. If the surface is uneven, the beam reacts differently. The particles scatter in all directions. So even if a surface is shiny, it is not a good reflector when the surface is uneven.

Flat mirrors are the best reflectors. The image seen in a mirror is reversed. The distance the object is from the mirror is the distance the image appears behind the mirror. Because of their surface, mirrors can easily change the direction of light. Because light bounces off at the same angle it enters, mirrors have multiple functions. Used in pairs, mirrors help to see beyond barriers and around corners by bending light. Submarine and toy periscopes work because

mirrors are parallel to each other and set at 45° angles. Periscopes work because the incoming light bounces to a second mirror. The light is then reflected to the eyes.

Curved Reflectors

Some mirrors are curved. Light reflects off a curved mirror much as it would if a series of flat mirrors were set at angles to each other. As the light particles hit each mirror, they bounce in many directions, but still at an equal angle to the incoming beam. With mirrors curved inward, the light rays can be reflected to a single spot, called a focal point. Curved mirrors focus light, making the light brighter and more intense. Flashlights, headlights, microscopes, and telescopes use curved mirrors.

Mirrors can curve in or out. Mirrors curved in, like the inside of a spoon, are called concave. The reflection from a concave mirror is larger because the light rays spread out. On the other hand, the outside of a spoon is an example of a convex mirror. It curves out, making an image look smaller. The convex mirror bends light, so the rays come together.

Color

Sir Isaac Newton was the first person to discover that light was actually comprised of a spectrum of seven colors: red, orange, yellow, green, blue, indigo, and violet. The spectrum stays in the same color order and can be easily remembered using the name ROY G BIV. Each color has a different wavelength. Red is the longest wavelength, and violet is the shortest. Since the photons travel at different speeds, they bend at different rates as they pass through a transparent object.

A prism is a triangular piece of glass commonly used to separate colors. Like a lens, light leaves the air and enters the prism, where it slows and bends. As it exits the glass and travels into the air, it bends again. Because the colors move in different wavelengths, they travel at different speeds. They bend at different degrees, resulting in a separation we can see.

Rainbows are created in a similar way, but the raindrops act like prisms. Sunlight enters the drop, and because of the drop's rounded shape, the sunlight reflects back to the front. As it leaves the drop, it bends again. The process causes the sunlight to spread out even more. With millions of drops refracting and reflecting sunlight, a rainbow appears.

Sound

Sound is a kind of energy made from vibrating objects. As an object begins to vibrate, the surrounding molecules also begin to move. Traveling in sound waves, the molecules collide with other objects in their path. The sound energy is transferred to those objects, so they, too, begin to vibrate. When the initial vibration stops, the sound stops. Vibrations can be heard, seen, and felt.

Anything that produces energy can make a sound. The wings of a bee move and create a vibration that produces a buzzing sound. A hammer hits a nail and produces a vibration from the contact. When we speak, air rushes out of the windpipe and collides with the vocal cords, tissues controlled by the muscles of the larynx. This collision causes the vocal cords to vibrate, resulting in sound. These sounds become words when the tongue, teeth, and lips shape the sounds.

Sound Waves

Sound waves are invisible. As the molecules move away in all directions, they travel in a concentric pattern. Their motion resembles the pattern made when a stone is tossed into water; as the circles move out, they get larger. But the energy diminishes as they grow.

Sound waves also travel through all matter, although at varying speeds. The only place sound energy cannot travel is in a vacuum. Most sounds we hear travel through air molecules, a gas. Since gas molecules are loosely packed, sound waves generally travel more slowly through air. The standard rate is 332 meters per second. However, the speed of travel increases with higher temperatures because the gas molecules are moving faster and colliding at an increased rate. When sound travels through water, it averages a speed of 1,433 meters per second. The hotter the liquid, the faster the sound wave travels. Sound waves travel faster through solids. In steel, they can travel 4,999 meters per second.

Loudness

Loudness is measured by the amplitude of a sound wave. Shorter amplitudes have a softer sound. Taller amplitudes have a louder sound. The faster and harder an object vibrates, the greater the amplitude of a wave will be, making the sound louder. High-pitched and low-pitched sounds can be soft or loud. Loudness is measured in units known as decibels. A soft sound, such as breathing, has a decibel reading of 0; it is barely audible. A jet plane's engine has a reading of 160 decibels, a level that is painful to human ears. Any sound that has a reading of more than 130 decibels is dangerous to human ears. Continuous exposure to sounds having high decibels can result in the loss of hearing.

Musical Instruments

Musical instruments produce sound waves in steady, regular intervals. A note is made of a sound that has the same pitch each time. The pitch is controlled by the material the instrument is made of as well as the size of it. A piccolo, having a high pitch, is a short, small-barreled instrument made of metal. A bassoon is a very long, hook-like instrument made of wood. There are three kinds of musical instruments: wind, string, and percussion. The instruments are grouped by the way the sounds are produced.

Wind instruments obtain their name because a player blows air from the mouth into the instrument. A thin wood piece, called a reed, produces the vibrations. Its vibrations travel the length of the instrument, which is filled with air, transferring its energy to the air molecules inside. The length of the air column is controlled by valves, which open to release air. When more holes are open, the air column is shorter. Thus, the pitch, or musical note, is higher. Flutes and recorders are examples of wind instruments.

Brass instruments are also included in the wind-instrument category. A player's lips vibrate to control the air flow into the instrument. It is the vibration of the lips that cause the energy to transfer to the air column in the instrument. French horns and tubas are brass instruments.

String instruments have strings. When plucked, hit, or moved with a bow, the strings vibrate. The vibrations are transferred to the surrounding air, thus producing sounds we can hear. Pitch, or the musical note, is made by changing the length of the strings. The piano, violin, and guitar are examples of string instruments.

In a percussion instrument, sound is made when a part of the instrument is hit, either by hand or with another object. That part of the instrument vibrates. The energy is transferred to the surrounding air so that the sound can be heard. The instrument is solid or constructed by stretching material over a hollow container. Cymbals and drums are percussion instruments.

RELATED READING

- *Flicker Flash* by Joan Bransfield Graham (Houghton Mifflin, 1999).
- *Hot and Cold* by Jack Challoner (*Start-Up Science Series*, Raintree Steck-Vaughn, 1996).
- *Hottest, Coldest, Highest, Deepest* by Steve Jenkins (Houghton Mifflin, 1998).
- *How Tall, How Short, How Faraway* by David A. Adler (Holiday House, 1999).
- *Light and Dark* by Jack Challoner (*Start-Up Science Series*, Raintree Steck-Vaughn, 1996).
- *Loud and Quiet* by Jack Challoner (*Start-Up Science Series*, Raintree Steck-Vaughn, 1996).
- *Pop! A Book About Bubbles* by Kimberley Brubaker Bradley (*Let's-Read-and-Find-Out Science Series*, HarperCollins, 2001).
- *Push and Pull* by Jack Challoner (*Start-Up Science Series*, Raintree Steck-Vaughn, 1996).
- *The Rainbow and You* by E. C. Krupp (HarperCollins, 2000).
- *The Science of Gravity* by John Stringer (*Science World Series*, Steck-Vaughn, 2000).
- *The Science of Noise* by Lynne Wright (*Science World Series*, Steck-Vaughn, 2000).
- *What Does a Wheel Do?* by Jim Pipe (Millbrook, 2002).

Unit 1 Assessment

 Read each sentence. Circle <u>true</u> or <u>false</u>.

1. Solids do not have a shape.   true   false

2. Milk is a liquid.   true   false

3. Temperature tells how much matter something has.   true   false

4. Water vapor is water in a gas form.   true   false

5. A mixture is made when you combine several things.   true   false

 What change is made in each picture? Write <u>shape</u>, <u>direction</u>, or <u>speed</u>.

6. _____   7. _____   8. _____

GO ON TO THE NEXT PAGE ☞

Unit 1 Assessment, p. 2

 Use a word from the box to complete each sentence.

high	air	reflects	gas
light	Sounds	bright	blocks

9. Air is a _____.

10. The Sun is a _____ light.

11. Light _____ off things we see.

12. You need _____ to make a shadow.

13. Something makes a shadow because it _____

the light.

14. _____ are made when things move back and

forth very fast.

15. A whistle is a _____ sound.

16. Sounds move to our ears through the _____.

Observing Matter

Everything in the world is made of **matter**. Matter is anything that takes up space and has **mass**. By observing matter, we can see its properties.

A **property** is a characteristic of an object. For example, the color yellow is a property of a banana. Sharpness is a property of scissors. Roundness is a property of an orange. All matter has properties.

Sort the matter in this picture by three different properties. List your groups below. Then, color the picture based on one of your groups. Use a different color for each property.

Property 1	Property 2	Property 3

Solids, Liquids, and Gases

Matter can be a **solid** like wood, a **liquid** like water, or a **gas** like air. Look at objects carefully. Then, you can decide their properties. You can tell what kind of matter they are.

You can see a solid. It holds its shape. You can see a liquid. It takes the shape of the container. However, you cannot see a gas. It takes the shape of the container.

Look at the pictures. Write <u>S</u> under the solids, <u>L</u> under the liquids, and <u>G</u> under the gases.

1. _____ 2. _____ 3. _____

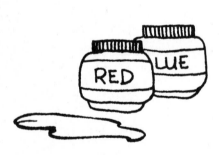

4. _____ 5. _____ 6. _____

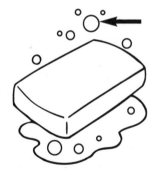

7. _____ 8. _____ 9. _____

Solids Have Shape

Solids have a definite shape.

 **Look at the pictures. Put an X on the picture in each row that is the same shape as the first picture in the row.**

1.          

2.          

3.       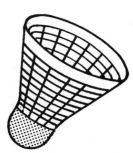

4.          

Wonderful Water

Water is an interesting kind of matter. It can be a solid, a liquid, or a gas. If water is a solid, it is ice. We can drink liquid water or use it in other ways. Water that is a gas is called **water vapor**.

Water can change from one form to another. If you freeze liquid water, it becomes a solid. If you melt the solid ice, it becomes a liquid. If you leave a glass of liquid water out without covering it, it evaporates and becomes a gas. This gas is invisible and is part of the air.

Draw lines to match the words on the left with the words on the right.

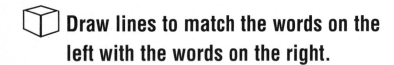

1. ice   liquid

2. water vapor   solid

3. water   gas

Air—Invisible Gas

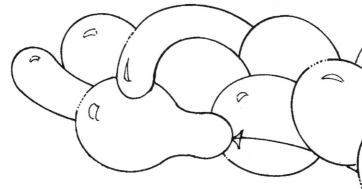

Is an empty cup <u>really</u> empty? What about an empty pocket? Or an empty lunch box? All of these things are really full. They are full of air.

Air is an invisible gas. Since we can't see it, we sometimes forget it is there. But it takes up space.

Air takes the shape of the container it is in. Think of a thin balloon and a round balloon. Since the balloons are different shapes, the air inside has different shapes.

Write a sentence about air.

_____

_____

_____

_____

_____

_____

Measuring Solids—Mass

We can measure the mass of matter. **Mass** means how much matter is in something. One way to measure mass is to balance one object with another object. When the balance tips, you know which object has more mass and which object has less mass. The side of the balance that is higher has less mass.

Circle the object that has more mass in each picture. It may not always be the bigger object!

1.

2.

3.

4.

Measuring Solids—Length

Matter can be measured. We can measure its **length**, or how long it is, and its height, or how tall it is.

Long ago, people measured objects by comparing them to something else. Many times they used parts of their bodies to measure against. For example, they might cut a piece of rope three hands long. But the lengths of people's hands were different. They found out that this was not a very accurate way to measure. If someone else cut the rope for them, it would be a different length.

Now, we measure objects in units that are the same size everywhere. That way, everyone knows exactly what size something is.

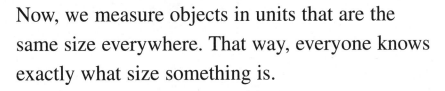

Measure the rope with your finger. Ask a friend to do the same thing.

Are the two measurements the same? _____

Measure some other objects with your friend. Complete the chart.

Object	Your Measure	Your Friend's Measure
1.		
2.		
3.		

Water Mass

Since water is matter, we know that it has mass. Do you think liquid water has the same mass as frozen water? To compare the two forms of water, we could use a balance. If the balance tips, we know that one form of water has more mass than the other. If the balance stays level, both forms of water have the same mass.

This picture shows a **balance**. There is one cup of liquid water on one side and one cup of water that has been frozen on the other side.

▢ Answer the question.

What do you observe about the mass of frozen water?

_____

_____

_____

_____

Changing Matter

Sometimes we want to change the shape of matter. We might change it by cutting it, bending it, or twisting it. Would this change its other properties? To find out, tear a corner off a sheet of paper. You have changed the paper's shape.

Circle <u>yes</u> or <u>no</u> to answer each question.

1. Is the sheet of paper still paper?   yes   no

2. Has its color changed?   yes   no

3. All together, is there still the same amount   yes   no
   of paper?

4. Can you change the shape of matter without   yes   no
   changing its other properties?

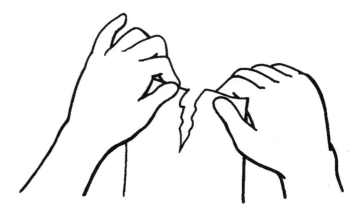

Another Change

You have probably made things from clay. You can break a lump of clay into pieces, slice it, or mold it. You can change its shape over and over. But it is still clay. Unless you throw away some clay, it will have the same mass, too.

The same thing is true about all kinds of matter. If you change the shape of the matter but keep all of the matter together when you measure it, its mass stays the same.

In the box draw something you could make from the clay.

Clay
5 ounces

Is the mass of your object different from the mass of the lump of clay?

_____

Mixtures

Have you ever made a mixture? You may have mixed a vegetable salad or fruit salad. You may have mixed up some clothes in a drawer. A **mixture** is made when you combine several things.

The things that go into a mixture can be separated. You can take the different vegetables or fruits out of a salad. They will be the same as they were before. You can sort out the clothes in the drawer. They will not have changed.

Look at the pictures. Separate the things in these mixtures. Draw them in different groups.

1.

2.

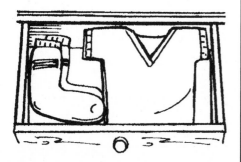

3.

Separating Dissolved Matter

If you have ever made salt water, you've made another kind of mixture. The salt is mixed into the water until it has **dissolved**. When something dissolves, it seems to disappear. It is still there, but the pieces of it are so small that they can't be seen.

Just like in mixtures of other things, the salt can be **separated** from the water. To do it, you would need to let the water **evaporate**. The salt would be left behind.

This is a picture of lemonade. Lemonade is a mixture of lemon juice, water, and sugar.

Write a sentence that tells a way to get the sugar out of lemonade.

_____

_____

_____

_____

_____

_____

What Is Temperature?

Temperature is the measure that tells how much heat there is. A higher temperature means there is more heat. A lower temperature means there is less heat. Do this activity to learn more about temperature.

You will need

☆ 2 bowls   ☆ 2 thermometers   ☆ warm water   ☆ ice

1. Fill one bowl with ice. Fill another bowl with warm water.

2. Put a thermometer in each bowl.

3. Look at the thermometers. What do you see?

Answer these questions on another sheet of paper.

1. What number did the liquid in each thermometer reach?

2. What do you think the temperature might be on a cold day?

3. What do you think it might be on a hot day?

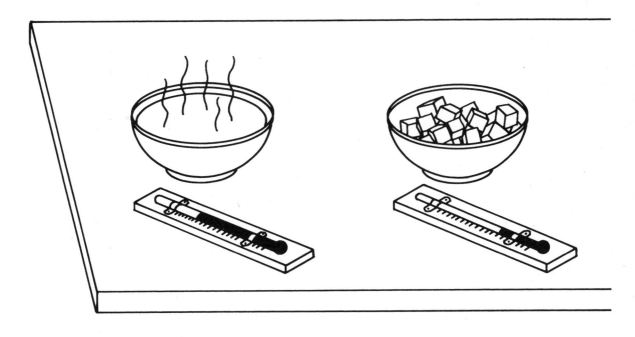

Measuring Temperature

Temperature is measured using a **thermometer**. Temperature can be measured in units called Fahrenheit or in units called Celsius. Scientists usually measure temperature in Celsius.

┌─ **You will need** ──────────┐
   ☆ a thermometer
└─────────────────────────────┘

Measure the air temperature in these places. Color each picture. Show how the thermometer looked. Write the temperature of each place.

On the floor   **Window ledge**   **Near the ceiling**   **Outside**

_____ °C   _____ °C   _____ °C   _____ °C

_____ °F   _____ °F   _____ °F   _____ °F

Heat Causes a Change

A **chemical change** occurs when heat changes something and it can't be changed back. If you add heat to popcorn kernels, they will turn into popcorn. Could you change the popcorn back to kernels again? If you add heat to bread, the bread turns into toast. Could you change the toast back into bread?

Draw what will happen if you add heat to these foods. Then, circle the changes that cannot be reversed.

1.

2.

3.

What Kind of Force?

A **force** is a push or pull.

 Label each picture <u>push</u> or <u>pull</u>. Draw an arrow to show the direction of the force.

1. _____

2. _____

3. _____

4. _____

5. _____

6. _____

What Forces Change a Shape?

A force is a push or pull. Force can change the shape of things. See how in this activity.

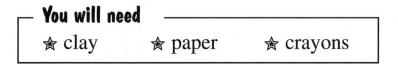

You will need

★ clay   ★ paper   ★ crayons

1. Roll the clay into a ball. Place the clay on the paper.

2. Push down on the clay ball. Trace around the clay.

3. Pull the clay with both hands. Trace around the clay.

Answer these questions on another sheet of paper.

1. How did the clay change shape when you pressed on it?

2. How did the clay change shape when you pulled on it?

3. Tell what forces you used to change the shape of the clay.

Pushes and Pulls

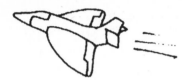

Things do not move on their own. It takes a force to move them. A force can start something moving. A force can change the direction that something is moving. A force can also make something stop moving.

A force is a push or pull. It takes a push to move a wheelbarrow or make an airplane fly. It takes a pull to move a wagon or a pull-toy.

📦 **Circle the toys you push. Color the toy you pull.**

1.

2.

3.

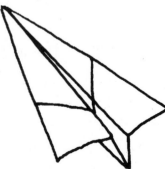

When Do You Need More Force?

A force is a push or pull. More force is needed to move things up a hill. You can show how in this activity.

> **You will need**
> - ⭐ board, 100 x 15 cm
> - ⭐ small, round object (paste bottle)
> - ⭐ 10 to 15 washers
> - ⭐ 3 books
> - ⭐ string
> - ⭐ paper cup

1. Tie one end of the string around the round object.

2. Tie the other end of the string to the cup.

3. Set the object on a table. Let the cup hang over the edge of the table.

4. Put washers in the cup, one at a time, until the cup begins to move.

5. Now, make a ramp from the books and board.

6. Place the object on the ramp. Repeat the activity.

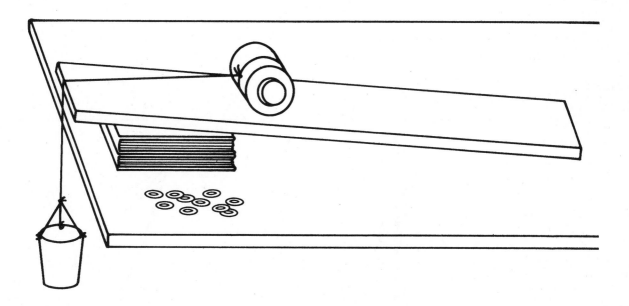

GO ON TO THE NEXT PAGE ☞

When Do You Need More Force?, p. 2

Answer the questions.

1. How many washers did it take to move the object on the table?

   _____

   _____

2. How many washers did it take to move the object up the ramp?

   _____

   _____

3. Is it easier to walk up or down a hill?

   _____

   _____

   _____

4. When do you need more force to move an object?

   _____

   _____

   _____

How Much Force?

A force is a push or pull. More force is needed to move things that are bigger or that weigh more. Show how in this activity.

You will need
☆ paper cup   ☆ string   ☆ crayons   ☆ 2 books

1. Tie one end of the string around one book.

2. Tie the other end of the string around the cup.

3. Set the book on the table. Let the cup hang over the edge of the table.

4. Put crayons in the cup, one at a time, until the cup begins to move.

5. Try the same activity using two books.

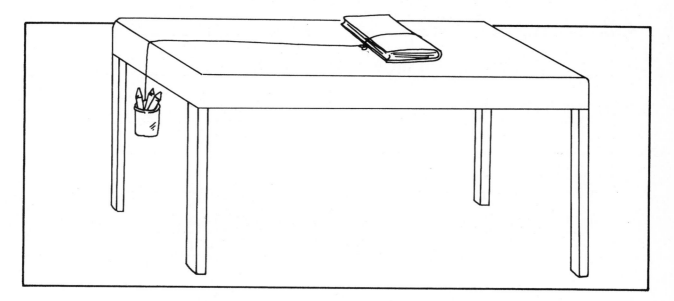

Answer these questions on another sheet of paper.

1. How many crayons did it take to move one book?

2. How many crayons did it take to move two books?

3. Would you need more force or less force to move a heavy box? Explain.

What Helps Things Move?

Friction is when two surfaces rub together. Friction makes it hard to move something. Learn more about friction in this activity.

> ### You will need
> ★ vegetable oil   ★ paper towels
> ★ powder   ★ 3 cups
> ★ sand

1. Pour a little oil, powder, or sand into each cup.

2. Rub two fingers together. Do they rub easily?

3. Dip one fingertip into the oil and remove it. Rub your fingers together. Do they feel rough or smooth? Clean your hands.

4. Record your answer in the chart on the next page.

5. Repeat the activity with the powder and sand.

GO ON TO THE NEXT PAGE ☞

What Helps Things Move?, p. 2

 Complete the chart. Mark an __X__ under the way each thing feels.

Material on Fingers	Rough	Smooth
Oil		
Powder		
Sand		

 Answer the questions.

1. When was it easier to slide your fingers?

_____

_____

_____

2. Tell which materials help things move more easily.

_____

_____

_____

3. When would it be good to have things move easily?

_____

_____

_____

How Do Surfaces Slow Things Down?

The **surface** of things can be rough or smooth. The surface can make things easier or harder to move. You can test different surfaces in this activity.

You will need
- ☆ block of wood
- ☆ sandpaper

1. Push a block of wood over the sandpaper.
   Is the block easy or hard to move? _____

2. Push a block of wood over a tile floor.
   Is the block easy or hard to move? _____

3. Push a block of wood over carpet.
   Is the block easy or hard to move? _____

4. Push a block of wood over a gym floor.
   Is the block easy or hard to move? _____

5. Push a block of wood over a sidewalk.
   Is the block easy or hard to move? _____

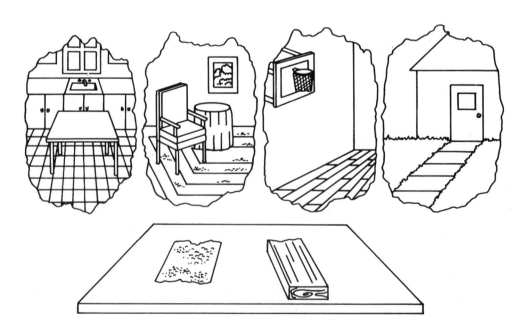

GO ON TO THE NEXT PAGE ☞

How Do Surfaces Slow Things Down?, p. 2

Answer the questions.

1. On which surfaces was it harder to push?

_____

_____

_____

2. On which surfaces was it easier to push?

_____

_____

3. Tell what kinds of surfaces slow things down.

_____

_____

4. When is it good for a surface to slow things down?

_____

_____

_____

Important Wheels

Some toys have **wheels** on them. Wheels make them easier to move. Wagons and wheelbarrows have wheels. Baby strollers and pull-toys do, too.

Make a list of things that have wheels.

_____

_____

_____

_____

_____

_____

_____

_____

The Pull of Gravity

Gravity is a force that pulls everything toward the ground—plants, animals, buildings, and objects. Gravity keeps things on Earth from floating off into space. It is the force that pulls you down a slide. It is the force that brings you back to Earth when you hop. The pull of gravity makes it hard for you to ride your bike up a hill. But it makes it easy for you to ride back down again. Earth's gravity is pulling on you all of the time.

📦 Look at the pictures. Tell what gravity is pulling in each picture.

1. _____

2. _____

3. _____

4. _____

Gravity and Weight

Gravity pulls you toward the ground, too. Just step on a scale. See how much you weigh. Your **weight** is a measure of the pull of gravity on your body.

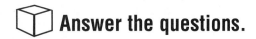 **Answer the questions.**

1. How much does Ei weigh?

_____ pounds

2. Ei and Jan are using a seesaw to see who weighs more. Which girl is heavier? Color her.

Light Makers

Some things make **light**.

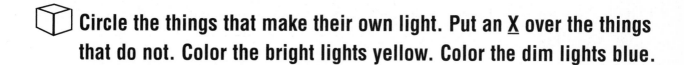 Circle the things that make their own light. Put an X over the things that do not. Color the bright lights yellow. Color the dim lights blue.

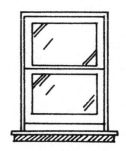

Name _____ Date _____

Do You Need Light To See?

The Sun is the way we get most of our light. At night, when there is no Sun, it is dark. Can you see in the dark? Try this activity to find out.

You will need
- ★ shoe box
- ★ crayon
- ★ scissors
- ★ masking tape
- ★ black construction paper

1. Cut a 1-inch (2.5-centimeter) hole in one end of the shoe box. Ask an adult for help if you need it.

2. Tape a crayon inside the other end of the box. Put the lid on the box.

3. Roll up the paper so it will fit in the hole.

4. Look in the box. What do you see?

5. Lift the lid a little. Now what do you see?

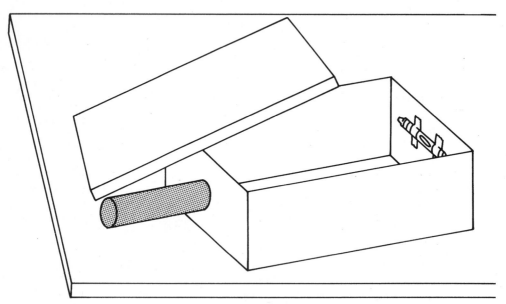

Answer these questions on another sheet of paper.

1. What did you see when the lid was closed?

2. What did you see when the lid was lifted?

3. Tell why you cannot see the crayon in the dark.

What Things Can Light Go Through?

Light can move through some things, such as a window. Some things block the light so it cannot go through, such as a book. Some things let a small amount of light through, such as wax paper. Test which things light will go through in this activity.

You will need
- ☆ different kinds of paper (writing, tissue, wax, grocery bags)
- ☆ different kinds of fabric (sheer, corduroy)
- ☆ colored cellophane
- ☆ aluminum foil
- ☆ window screen
- ☆ other things to test

1. Choose five things. Write the names of your choices in the chart on the next page.

2. Guess if the thing will let light go through. Write your guess in the chart.

3. Hold up each thing to the light. Did light go through? Write what you found out in the chart.

GO ON TO THE NEXT PAGE ☞

What Things Can Light Go Through?, p. 2

🔲 **Complete the chart.**

WHICH THINGS LET LIGHT THROUGH?

Thing	My Guess	What I Found Out

🔲 **Answer the questions.**

1. Which things let light through?

_____

_____

2. Which things did not?

_____

_____

3. List some activities that you need light for.

_____

_____

_____

How Can Light Go Around a Corner?

Light moves in a straight line. As it gets farther away from its source, it spreads out. The light gets dimmer. Because light moves in a straight line, you must use mirrors to see around corners. See why in this activity.

You will need

★ flashlight   ★ small mirror

Safety First: Some mirrors have sharp corners and break easily. Handle the mirror carefully.

1. Work in groups of three students.
   Have one person stand away from each corner.
   Have a third person stand at the corner.

2. Turn on the flashlight.
   Shine it straight ahead.
   Does the light go around
   the corner?

3. Have the person at the
   corner hold a mirror.
   Get the person to move the
   mirror to make the light go
   around the corner.

GO ON TO THE NEXT PAGE ☞

How Can Light Go Around a Corner?, p. 2

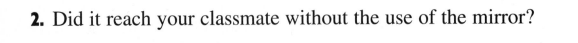 **Answer the questions.**

1. Did the light reach your classmate with the use of the mirror?

_____

_____

2. Did it reach your classmate without the use of the mirror?

_____

_____

3. Tell what the mirror did to the light.

_____

_____

_____

4. Find out what a periscope is. How does it use mirrors?

_____

_____

_____

_____

Name _____   Date _____

What Will Make a Good Reflector?

When light hits something, it bounces off in another direction. This bouncing is called **reflection**. Learn more about reflection in this activity.

You will need
★ flashlight   ★ mirror   ★ 2 squares of foil

1. Ball up one sheet of foil. Then, flatten it out.

2. Hold the mirror in one hand and the flashlight in the other. Stand next to a wall. Shine the light on the mirror. Move the mirror until you make a reflection on the wall. What do you see?

3. Repeat Step 2 using the smooth foil. What do you see?

4. Repeat Step 2 using the crumpled foil. What do you see?

Answer these questions on another sheet of paper.

1. Which thing made the best reflection?

2. What was the surface like?

3. What kind of surface makes a good reflector?

4. How do bicycle reflectors keep you safe at night?

Do Shadows Made by the Sun Change?

A **shadow** is made because something blocks light. Find out more about shadows in this activity.

You will need

★ meter stick   ★ chalk

1. Go outside on a sunny morning.
   Ask a friend to trace your shadow.

2. Measure the length of your shadow.
   Write the number in the chart on the next page.

3. Go outside in the afternoon.
   Stand in the same place.
   Ask a friend to trace your shadow again.

4. Measure the length of your shadow.
   Write the number in the chart.

GO ON TO THE NEXT PAGE ☞

Do Shadows Made by the Sun Change?, p. 2

Complete the chart.

SHADOW MEASUREMENT

Time	Length
Morning	
Afternoon	

Answer the questions.

1. How long was your shadow in the morning?

_____

2. How long was it in the afternoon?

_____

3. Did your shadow change in other ways?

_____

_____

_____

4. What made your shadow change?

_____

_____

What Colors Are in Light?

A **prism** is a triangle made of glass or plastic. When light passes through the prism, the light bends. A rainbow is made when the light bends. See how a prism works in this activity.

You will need
- ☆ prism   ☆ white paper   ☆ tape   ☆ flashlight or sunlight
- ☆ crayons (red, yellow, blue, green, orange, violet, purple)

---

1. Tape the white paper to a wall.

2. Hold the flashlight in one hand.
   Put the prism on a table in front of the paper.

3. Shine the light on the prism.
   Move the flashlight so the light will shine on the paper.

   What do you see? _____

   _____

4. Draw the order of the colors in the box on the next page.

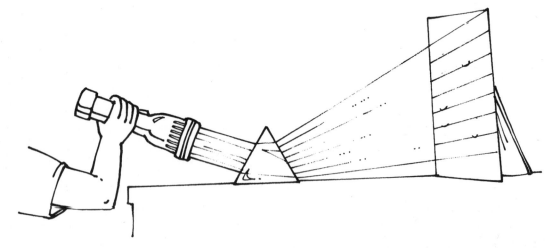

GO ON TO THE NEXT PAGE ☞

What Colors Are in Light?, p. 2

 **In the box draw the rainbow of colors that you saw during the activity.**

RAINBOW OF COLORS

 **Answer the questions.**

1. What is the order of the colors?

_____

_____

2. How did the prism help to make the rainbow?

_____

_____

3. Do the colors of the rainbow change? Explain.

_____

_____

Can You Make Sound?

Sound is made when something moves up and down very quickly. This kind of movement is called a **vibration**. Learn about making sounds in this activity.

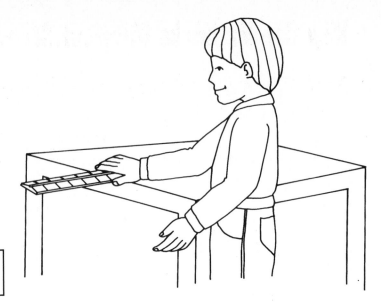

┌─ **You will need** ─────────────┐
★ 12-in. (30-cm) plastic ruler

1. Put a ruler on the desk. Hold the ruler in place so that half of it hangs off the edge of the desk.

2. Gently snap the end of the ruler that hangs off the desk.

   What do you see? _____

   What do you hear? _____

3. Snap the ruler again, but do it harder.

   What do you see? _____

   What do you hear? _____

4. Move the ruler so that 8 inches (20 cm) of the ruler hang off the desk. Repeat Steps 2 and 3.

Answer these questions on another sheet of paper.

1. How did the ruler move when you snapped it?
2. How did the sound of the ruler change when you snapped it harder?
3. How did the sound change when more of the ruler stuck out?
4. How are sounds made?

How Can You Make Different Sounds?

Some sounds are loud. Other sounds are soft. Some sounds are high, and some are low. Make different sounds in this activity.

You will need

☆ plastic ruler   ☆ rubber band   ☆ pencil

Safety First: Be careful as you do this activity. The rubber band may slip. The ruler could fly off the table.

1. Put a rubber band around the long side of the ruler.

2. Put the pencil under the rubber band. Put one finger on the pencil to hold the rubber band down.

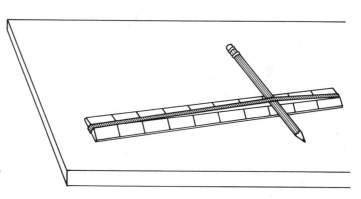

3. Snap the rubber band gently. Snap it harder.

   What do you hear?

_____

4. Move the pencil to different parts of the ruler. Snap the rubber band.

📦 **Answer these questions on another sheet of paper.**

1. When did the sound change?

2. Tell how you can make a louder or softer sound.

3. Tell how you can make a higher or lower sound.

Name _____ Date _____

Does Sound Travel Better Through Cotton or Air?

Sound can travel through many things. It can move through water, air, and the ground. It travels through some things better than others. Learn more in this activity.

You will need

★ 2 self-sealing plastic bags   ★ cotton   ★ alarm clock that ticks

1. Fill one bag with cotton. Seal the bag.

2. Fill one bag with air. Seal the bag.

3. Hold the bag with cotton next to your ear.

4. Ask a friend to hold the clock next to the bag.

   What do you hear? _____

5. Hold the bag with air next to your ear. Repeat Step 4.

Answer these questions on another sheet of paper.

1. When was the sound louder?

2. Does sound travel better through cotton or air?

3. What other things is it hard for sound to travel through?

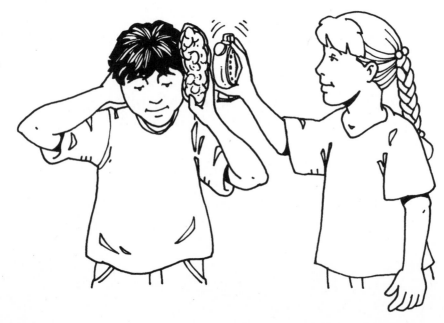

High and Low Sounds

Some sounds are high. Some sounds are low. You can make different sounds in this activity.

You will need

★ 3 glasses   ★ water   ★ ruler

---

1. Put 3 centimeters of water in one glass.

2. Put 6 centimeters of water in another glass.

3. Put 9 centimeters in the last glass.

4. Tap each glass with a spoon. Be careful.

   Which glass makes the lowest sound? _____

   Which makes the highest sound? _____

Write <u>high</u>, <u>low</u>, or <u>medium</u> under each glass.

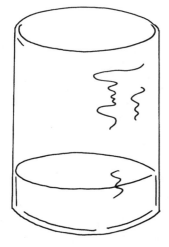 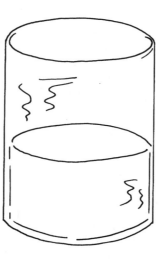 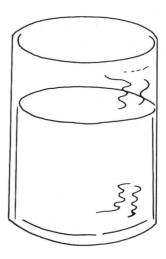

1. _____   2. _____   3. _____

How Do People Make Vocal Sounds?

Your **lungs** push air up into your throat. Two muscles, called **vocal cords**, vibrate when the air passes across them.

Safety First: Do not push on your throat too hard.

1. Put your hand on your throat.

2. Hum softly. Then, hum more loudly.

3. Make other sounds or words.

 **Answer these questions on another sheet of paper.**

1. What do you feel when you hum softly?

2. What do you feel when you hum more loudly?

3. What do you feel when you make other sounds?

4. What happens in your throat to make sounds?

Guitars

A **guitar** makes sound when a string is plucked. You can make a guitar in this activity.

You will need
- ☆ milk carton
- ☆ rubber band
- ☆ 2 pencils

1. Stretch the rubber band around the carton.

   Put the two pencils under the rubber band.

2. Ask a friend to put a finger on each pencil.

   Pluck the string. Is the sound high or low? _____

3. Move the pencils apart. Repeat Step 2.

   Is the sound high or low? _____

⬛ **Circle the guitar that is making the higher sound.**

Echoes

Echoes are made when sounds bounce off things.

1. Find a building with a large, flat wall.

2. Take about 100 giant steps away from the wall.

3. Stand facing the wall. Clap your hands. Do you hear an echo?

4. Make other sounds and see if you can hear echoes.

A room that echoes can be very noisy. Soft materials on floors, walls, and ceilings cut down noise. Look around the room. Name some things that might cut noise in your classroom.

_____

_____

_____

_____

Are Two Ears Better Than One?

Your ears help you to hear sounds. Can you hear better with one ear or two ears? Try this activity to find out.

> **You will need**
> ☆ a blindfold   ☆ 2 pencils

1. Ask a friend to help you. Put on the blindfold. Have your friend stand 10 feet (3 meters) away.

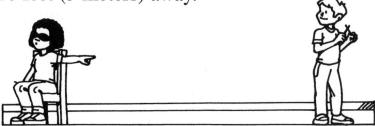

2. Have your friend tap the pencils together. Point to where the sound came from.

3. Have your friend move somewhere else in the room five other times. Repeat Step 2. Did you point in the right direction?

4. Now, plug one ear. Repeat Step 3.

📦 **Answer these questions on another sheet of paper.**

1. How many times did you point in the right direction when you used two ears?

2. How many times did you point in the right direction when you used one ear?

3. Can you hear better with two ears or one ear? Explain.

Unit 2: Earth and Space Science

BACKGROUND INFORMATION

The Earth is made up of three materials: solids, liquids, and gases. The solids inside the Earth are such things as minerals, rocks, and soil. The liquid with which we are most familiar is water. But the Earth also has liquid metal and rock under its surface. And various gases, mostly oxygen and nitrogen, make up the atmosphere that allows life on the Earth.

The Earth

The Earth has a diameter of about 8,000 miles (12,900 km) and a circumference of about 25,000 miles (40,250 km). The Earth is made up of three layers. The outer layer of the Earth, called the crust, is quite thin, ranging from 3 to 34 miles (5–55 km) thick. We live on the crust, and most of the rocks and minerals we recognize come from the crust.

Below the crust is the mantle. The mantle is about 1,800 miles (2,900 km) thick, and it is made of mostly solid rock. The mantle is very hot, up to 5,400°F (3,000°C). Below the mantle is the core. The core is about 2,200 miles (3,500 km) thick, and it has a temperature as high as 7,200°F (4,000°C). Most scientists think the core has two parts, an outer core and an inner core. The outer core is made of melted iron and nickel. The inner core is a solid ball of iron and nickel.

Minerals and Rocks

Rocks are made up of minerals. Minerals have four characteristics that classify them as minerals. 1. They are substances that occur naturally. 2. They are inorganic solids. 3. Minerals of the same type usually have the same chemical composition. 4. The atoms of minerals are arranged in a regular pattern that forms crystals.

Rocks are classified into three basic groups: igneous, sedimentary, and metamorphic. These groups are based on how the rock is formed.

Igneous rocks begin as molten rock, a red-hot liquid. *Igneous* means "fire," so igneous rocks can be called "fire rocks." After a long while, the molten rock cools and hardens to form solid rock. The hardening can occur on the surface or below the surface of the Earth. Molten rock that is on the surface of the Earth is called lava. Granite is an example of igneous rock.

Sedimentary rocks are made up of sediments, or bits of rock and sand. The sediments piled up to form layers. The weight of the layers squeezed the sediments. Chemicals in the sediments cemented them together. The squeezing and cementing eventually caused the sediments to harden into layers of rock. Sandstone is an example of sedimentary rock.

Sometimes rocks that have already formed become buried deep in the Earth. There, great pressures inside the Earth squeeze the rocks. Great heat makes the rocks very hot but does not melt them. The squeezing and heat slowly change these rocks from one kind to another. The new kind of rock is called a metamorphic rock. *Metamorphic* means "changed." Igneous, sedimentary, and even other metamorphic rocks can be changed to form new metamorphic rocks. Slate is an example of metamorphic rock. Slate is formed from the sedimentary rock shale.

Soil

Soil is the grainy material that covers much of the land on the Earth. Soil is made of tiny bits of rock, minerals, organic materials, water, and air. Soil is needed for life to exist on the Earth. Plants need soil to grow. Then, animals, including people, eat the plants to stay alive.

Soil is created through a long process. Rocks break down through weathering and erosion into a stony product called parent soil. This type of soil is broken down further, mostly through weathering. Organic matter called humus mixes with the parent soil. When the long process is complete, the rock bits and humus have mixed to produce fertile soil, which is good for growing plants.

Weathering and Erosion

The Earth's surface undergoes constant change. Any process that causes rocks or landforms to break down is called weathering. Weathering is caused by several agents, including water, wind, ice, and plants. Weathering is usually a slow process, causing the gradual deterioration of the rocks or landforms.

Erosion is another way in which rocks and landforms are broken down or worn away. Erosion is the process in which weathered rock and soil are moved from one place to another. The most effective agents of erosion are moving water, waves, gravity, wind, and glaciers.

Fossils

A fossil is the preserved remains of a thing that was once alive, usually a plant or an animal. These remains are found in rock layers, so that if scientists know how old the rocks are, they can tell how old the plant or animal is. Scientists who study fossils are called paleontologists.

Most fossils form from a bone or a shell. Some fossils, though, mark the burrow or track of an animal; these are called trace fossils. Most fossils are found in sedimentary rock. But fossils have also been found in asphalt, frozen ice, and tree resin.

Water

Water is our most precious resource. Water covers about 70 percent of the Earth's surface. Without water, life could not exist. Our bodies are about 65 percent water. We use water in many ways. Water is an amazing substance, too. It can be a solid, a liquid, and a gas. It can change from a solid state (ice) to a liquid state (water) to a gaseous state (water vapor) and back again.

The Water Cycle

Water often changes from its liquid form to its gaseous form and back to its liquid form in a process called the water cycle. The three main steps in the water cycle are evaporation, condensation, and precipitation. Evaporation is necessary to get the liquid water into its gaseous form of water vapor in the air. Condensation is needed to turn the vapor back to a liquid in the clouds. And precipitation returns the liquid water to the Earth.

Evaporation occurs as liquid water is heated and changed into water vapor. The water vapor is then carried up into the sky by rising air. Condensation takes place as the rising water vapor cools and is changed into liquid water, forming clouds. Precipitation happens as water droplets grow heavy and fall to the Earth as rain, snow, or some other type of precipitation.

Gases and the Atmosphere

We live on the crust of the Earth. We have food and water. But another part of the Earth's structure is necessary to sustain life. That part is called the atmosphere. The atmosphere is made up of various gases, mostly nitrogen and oxygen, that allow us to survive on the Earth. The atmosphere is about 500 miles (800 km) high, and it is held in place by the Earth's gravity.

The atmosphere has four layers. Closest to the Earth is the troposphere, the layer in which we live. The troposphere is only a thin band, about five to ten miles (8–16 km) thick. All the Earth's weather occurs in the troposphere. The troposphere also contains the air we need to live. The air in the troposphere is about 80 percent nitrogen and 20 percent oxygen. There are also small amounts of other gases, including argon and carbon dioxide.

Above the troposphere is the stratosphere, a layer that is from about five to 50 miles (8–80 km) high. The stratosphere has only a few clouds, which are mostly made of ice crystals. In the stratosphere are the fast-moving winds known as the jet stream. The air in the lower part of the stratosphere is cold. In the upper part of the stratosphere, the temperature increases. The important ozone layer is in the upper stratosphere. The ozone absorbs ultraviolet energy from the Sun, which causes the temperature there to rise. The ozone layer is important because it protects creatures on the Earth from the harmful ultraviolet rays.

Above the stratosphere is the ionosphere, which stretches from about 50 miles to about 300 miles (80–500 km) above the Earth. There is almost no air in the ionosphere. But the ionosphere is useful for communication with satellites and radio astronomy. The natural displays of light called auroras occur in the ionosphere.

The top layer of the atmosphere is called the exosphere. It begins about 300 miles (500 km) above the Earth, but it has no definite top boundary. This layer is the beginning of what we call outer space. The exosphere contains mostly oxygen and helium gases. This layer also has a very high temperature, up to several thousand degrees.

Weather

Weather, in its most basic explanation, is caused by the uneven heating of the Earth's surface by the Sun. The land and the water are heated differently. This uneven heating causes pockets of air with different temperatures. Cool air is heavier than warm air. As a result, the cooler air moves under the warmer air, so the lighter warm air is pushed up. This movement of air causes winds. These factors all work together to produce weather.

We live in the layer of the Earth's atmosphere called the troposphere. Air in the troposphere moves constantly. The air is heated, not directly by the Sun, but by the air's contact with the Earth. Air closer to the Earth is warmer than air higher up. Cold air is heavier than warm air, so the cold air moves downward. The warm air rises as it is displaced, setting up the patterns of air circulation in the troposphere.

Near the Earth's surface, the sinking air results in high-pressure zones called ridges. The rising air creates low-pressure zones called troughs. The differences in air pressure produce winds. Wind moves out of high-pressure zones in a clockwise direction and into low-pressure zones in a counterclockwise direction. Weather data identifies winds by the direction from which they come. For example, a wind moving toward the south is called a north wind, because north is the direction from which it comes.

Great air masses move slowly across the Earth's surface. These moving air masses take on the characteristics of the surface beneath them. Air moving over a warm surface is warmed, and air moving over a cold surface is cooled. Air moving over water becomes moist, and air moving over land becomes drier. As it moves, the air mass causes changes in the weather of an area.

Fronts

A front is a line or boundary between air masses. The air masses clash along the front, so weather along a front is often stormy. A cold front occurs when a cold air mass replaces a warm air mass. Weather along a cold front often includes thunderstorms with much precipitation. A warm front occurs when a warm air mass replaces a cold air mass. Precipitation may also occur along a warm front, but the precipitation is usually not as heavy as along a cold front. A stationary front occurs when air masses meet without moving. A stationary front may produce an extended period of precipitation.

Precipitation

Precipitation is one of the most obvious features of weather. As you recall, precipitation is the third step in the water cycle, following evaporation and condensation. Sometimes precipitation does not fall in an area for a long period of time. Plants and crops can die, and sometimes even animals and people die as a result of the lack of water. When an area does not receive precipitation for a long time, it is said to be in a drought.

Clouds

Another of the most obvious, and sometimes most spectacular, features of weather is the cloud. Clouds can take several forms, from thin and wispy to dense and billowy. How do clouds form? Remember the movement of air, with warm air rising as the cold air sinks? First, through evaporation, water on the Earth's surface becomes water vapor in the air. As the warm air rises and expands, it naturally begins to cool. Water vapor in the air starts to condense around tiny particles in the air, such as dust or smoke, forming droplets. Clouds form in different shapes, depending on their height, the coolness of the air, and the amount of water vapor in the air.

The water droplets grow bigger as more water vapor condenses. When the droplets get so large they cannot be held up by the rising air, they fall as rain or some other form of precipitation. If the cloud is cold and contains crystals of ice, snow may fall instead of rain.

There are three main types of clouds: cirrus, cumulus, and stratus. Cirrus clouds are high above the Earth and are usually seen in fair weather. These clouds, made of ice crystals, are wispy and streak the sky. Cumulus clouds are white and fluffy, looking much like cotton balls. They are often seen in good weather, though they can produce rain showers or snow. Stratus clouds are low, dark clouds close to the Earth. They often produce rain or snow.

Stormy Weather

Weather comes in many forms, fair and foul. Fair weather includes sunny days, gentle breezes, and mild temperatures. But foul weather is more spectacular, accompanied as it often is by powerful displays of wind, rain, lightning, and thunder. One of the most common examples of foul weather is the thunderstorm. Approaching thunderstorms are often accompanied by towering cumulus clouds called thunderheads. These billowy clouds have flat tops and dark bottoms. Thunderheads are formed when warm, moist air rises. As the rising air begins to cool, water vapor in the air condenses, and cumulus clouds form. The hot ground causes the heated air to rise faster and higher. The cumulus clouds grow larger and taller, often reaching ten miles or more into the air. As the clouds grow in size, they become more likely to produce rain.

Thunderheads also produce two well-known features of stormy weather: lightning and thunder. Lightning is an electrical spark caused by friction inside the thunderhead. As the clouds grow, raindrops scrape against each other, and friction is produced. This friction builds up an electrical charge, just as you do when you scrape your feet across a carpet. Most of the electric charges in the lower part of the cloud are negative. These negative charges emit a spark that jumps toward a positive charge on the ground. This spark is what we call lightning. The lightning instantly heats the air around its path. This heated air expands quickly and collides with cooler air. The collision between the heated air and the cooler air produces the sound we know as thunder.

The Sun

Life on the Earth begins with the Sun, and the Earth's weather is also caused by the Sun and its energy. The Sun produces energy in the form of heat and light. In the center of the Sun, its core, nuclear fusion reactions change hydrogen into helium. These reactions release an unbelievable amount of energy. At the core, the Sun burns at a temperature of about 27 million degrees F (15 million degrees C). The energy moves from the core to the surface of the Sun, which has a temperature of almost 4 million degrees F (2.2 million degrees C). The energy then travels through space as electromagnetic waves of light and heat.

The Earth is 93 million miles (150 million km) from the Sun, so only a tiny amount of the Sun's energy reaches the Earth. But this small amount is enough to sustain life and create weather on the Earth. Much of the Sun's energy and harmful rays are filtered out by the Earth's atmosphere. About half of the Sun's energy is absorbed or reflected by the ozone, clouds, or the air. About 50 percent is absorbed by the Earth's surface.

The Sun is much larger than the Earth, with a diameter of about 840,000 miles (1,352,000 km), compared to the Earth's diameter of about 8,000 miles (12,900 km). But the Sun is, in fact, only a medium-sized star. Many early people believed that the Sun moved around the Earth, but the opposite is true. The Earth orbits around the Sun, once every 365 days or 1 year.

The Solar System

The Earth joins eight other planets in the solar system. These nine planets orbit around the Sun. (Recent research by astronomers suggests there may be a tenth planet somewhere beyond Pluto.) The planets all receive energy from the Sun, but they receive varying amounts based on their distance from the Sun. The inner planets (Mercury, Venus, Earth, Mars) receive more energy because they are closer. The outer planets (Jupiter, Saturn, Uranus, Neptune, Pluto) are very cold planets where the chance of life is very small. Students can remember the order of the planets outward from the Sun by using this saying: "My Very Energetic Mother Just Sent Us Nine Pizzas."

The other planets are mostly quite different from the Earth. The planet closest to the Sun, Mercury, has a year, or one orbit of the Sun, that is only 88 Earth days long. On Mercury, the surface temperature can be as low as about –290°F (–173°C) or as high as 800°F (425°C). For the most distant planet, Pluto, one orbit takes 248 Earth years. Pluto is about three billion miles (4.8 billion km) from the Sun. On Neptune, winds sometimes blow up to 700 miles per hour (1,125 km per hour).

The planets are held in their orbits by the Sun's gravitational pull. Likewise, the Earth and the farther planets have smaller bodies, or moons, that orbit around them, held by each planet's gravitational pull. The Earth has one moon. On the other hand, Jupiter has at least 17 moons.

The Moon

The Moon is a satellite of the Earth. It is about one fourth the size of the Earth, with a diameter of about 2,100 miles (3,400 km). The Moon appears about the same size as the Sun in the sky, but that is only because the Moon is so much closer than the Sun. The Moon is about 240,000 miles (384,000 km) from the Earth, and the Sun is about 93 million miles (150 million km). The Moon orbits the Earth once about every 29 days.

The Moon has no light of its own, but it seems to shine because it reflects the Sun's light. The Moon also has no atmosphere and no life. The Moon's gravity is only about one sixth as strong as the Earth's gravity. A person who weighs 60 pounds (27 kilograms) on the

Earth would weigh only 10 pounds (4.5 kilograms) on the Moon!

Meteors

Have your students ever seen a "shooting star"? Shooting stars are not really stars; this is just a popular name for meteors. Comets leave behind a trail of dust and gas, also called meteoroids, as they pass through the solar system. When the Earth moves through these dust particles, they appear in the atmosphere as meteors. Because most meteors are no bigger than a grain of sand, they burn up quickly in a flash of light. If a meteor is large enough, it may survive its dive and hit the surface of the Earth. Then, the surviving chunk of rock is called a meteorite.

The Earth passes through the same fields of comet dust every year. This passage produces yearly showers of meteors, from several to hundreds of meteors per hour. Some of the more spectacular meteor showers are the Quadrantids on January 3, the Perseids on August 12, and the Geminids on December 14.

Stars

Stars are great balls of gas that burn at tremendous temperatures. They undergo a nuclear fusion reaction that changes hydrogen to helium. Our Sun is the nearest star. Most stars are very, very far away. Stars are very, very bright, but they seem dim to us because of their great distance, like a burning match many miles away. Stars are so far away from the Earth that their distances are measured in light-years. A light-year is the distance it takes light (moving at 186,000 miles per second or 300,000 kilometers per second) to travel in one year. Stars differ from one another in their color, brightness, and size. One of the brighter stars seen from the Earth is Polaris, also known as the North Star.

Some stars appear grouped in recognizable shapes. These groups are called constellations. Most constellations were named by ancient people. Some constellations are Orion, Leo, Scorpius, and Ursa Major, also called the Great Bear. The Big Dipper is part of Ursa Major. Constellations are noted on star charts, which are like maps of the sky. On a clear night, about 6,000 stars are visible to the unaided eye.

A larger grouping of stars is called a galaxy. Galaxies contain billions of stars, and there are billions of galaxies in the universe. Our solar system is in the Milky Way galaxy. On a clear, dark night, away from city lights, the Milky Way is visible as a sparkling band across the vault of the sky.

Rotation of the Earth

The Earth moves constantly, rotating on its axis, which causes the day and night cycle. The Earth also revolves around the Sun and tilts on its axis. As the tilt changes, parts of the Earth are closer to the Sun. The seasons occur as a result of the Earth's tilt on its axis. During the six months that the North Pole is tilted toward the Sun, the Northern Hemisphere gets more sunlight than the Southern Hemisphere does. The atmosphere then is warmer in the Northern Hemisphere, resulting in warmer weather. During the time the North Pole is tilted toward the Sun, the Northern Hemisphere experiences late spring, summer, and early fall. At the same time, the Southern Hemisphere is having late fall, winter, and early spring. The Northern Hemisphere experiences these later seasons when the North Pole is tilted away from the Sun.

Studying the Skies

A place that gives shows about the stars and planets is called a planetarium. You can make a simple planetarium with a flashlight and an oatmeal box or frozen juice can. Carefully punch the shape of a constellation in the end of the box or can. Then, in a dark room, shine the flashlight inside the box or can and project the constellation on the wall or ceiling.

Scientists who study the sky and its objects are called astronomers. Astronomers use telescopes and radio waves to study the galaxies and the universe. Astronomers work in places called observatories. Two famous observatories are Palomar Observatory in California and McDonald Observatory in Texas. Astronomers can also use the Hubble Space Telescope to see even farther into space.

What lies beyond? Is there life on other worlds? No one really knows. But a familiarity with our neighbors in the sky will help students to find their own place in the greater scheme of things.

RELATED READING

- *Cloud Dance* by Thomas Locker (Harcourt, 2000).

- *The Earth* by Tim Furniss (*Spinning Through Space Series*, Steck-Vaughn, 2001).

- *First Step Weather Series* by Robin Nelson (Lerner, 2001).

- *The International Space Station* by Franklyn M. Branley (*Let's-Read-and-Find-Out Science Series*, HarperCollins, 2000).

- *Our Big Home: An Earth Poem* by Linda Glaser (Millbrook, 2000).

- *The Solar System* by Tim Furniss (*Spinning Through Space Series*, Steck-Vaughn, 2001).

- *Water Dance* by Thomas Locker (Harcourt Brace, 1997).

- *Weather Around You* by Angela Royston (*Geography Starts Here Series*, Raintree Steck-Vaughn, 1998).

Unit 2 Assessment

Read each sentence. Circle true or false.

1. The Earth has ten layers.   true   false

2. Water changes rocks.   true   false

3. Rocks can break down into small pieces.   true   false

4. A fossil is made of wood.   true   false

5. Dinosaurs live on Earth today.   true   false

6. All soils are the same.   true   false

7. You should stay inside during a thunderstorm.   true   false

8. Thermometers measure wind speed.   true   false

9. The Earth is the closest planet to the Sun.   true   false

10. The Earth rotates twice each day.   true   false

GO ON TO THE NEXT PAGE 👉

Unit 2 Assessment, p. 2

Darken the letter of the answer that best completes the sentence.

11. Air is an invisible _____.
Ⓐ solid
Ⓑ liquid
Ⓒ gas

12. The top layer of the Earth is called the _____.
Ⓐ core
Ⓑ crust
Ⓒ mantle

13. When rocks rub against each other, they get _____.
Ⓐ bigger
Ⓑ harder
Ⓒ smaller

14. _____ are hardened shapes of plants and animals.
Ⓐ Liquids
Ⓑ Fossils
Ⓒ Dinosaurs

15. _____ are made of tiny drops of water.
Ⓐ Clouds
Ⓑ Fossils
Ⓒ Rocks

16. Clouds help us know what the _____ will be.
Ⓐ weather
Ⓑ erosion
Ⓒ degrees

17. The _____ revolves around the Earth.
Ⓐ Sun
Ⓑ Moon
Ⓒ Mars

18. The _____ moves around the Sun.
Ⓐ shadow
Ⓑ Earth
Ⓒ wind

19. _____ is the largest planet.
Ⓐ Earth
Ⓑ Mars
Ⓒ Jupiter

20. A group of stars is called a _____.
Ⓐ cloud
Ⓑ constellation
Ⓒ planet

The Earth

The Earth is our home. How much do you know about the Earth?

Read each sentence. Which word makes the sentence true? Darken the letter by the correct answer.

1. The land is made of rock and _____.

   Ⓐ air   Ⓑ soil   Ⓒ Sun

2. Most of the Earth is covered by _____.

   Ⓐ grass   Ⓑ woods   Ⓒ water

Color the Earth below.

Color 1 green. This is land.

Color 2 blue. This is water.

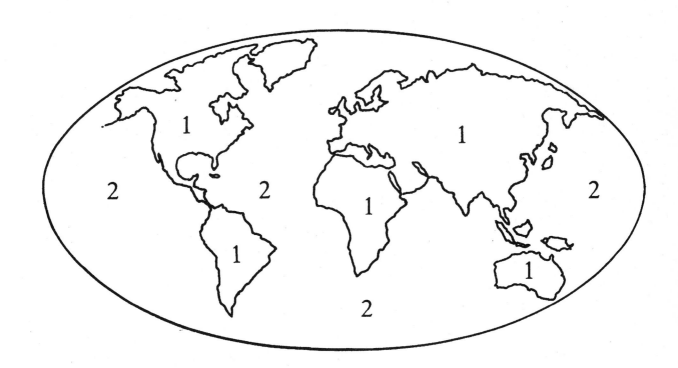

Name _____ Date _____

Inside the Earth

The Earth is like a giant ball. It is made of three layers. The center of the Earth is called the **core**. It is very hot. The middle layer is called the **mantle**. It is wrapped around the core. The core heats the mantle. The mantle becomes so hot that some rocks in this layer melt. The mantle is so deep that people have not seen it. The outer layer is called the **crust**. It is solid and thinner than the other layers. The crust is made of rock and soil. We live on the crust of the Earth. Learn more about the Earth's layers in this activity.

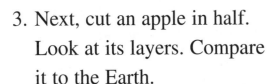

You will need
☆ apple   ☆ hard-boiled egg   ☆ knife

1. Look at the picture below of the Earth's layers.

2. Cut a hard-boiled egg in half. Look at the layers. Compare it to the Earth.

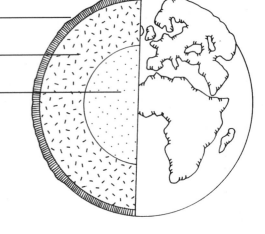

a. _____

b. _____

c. _____

3. Next, cut an apple in half. Look at its layers. Compare it to the Earth.

 **Answer the questions.**

1. Label the three layers of the Earth in the picture.

2. How are the egg and the Earth alike?

_____

_____

3. How are the apple and the Earth alike?

_____

Kinds of Rocks

There are many kinds of **rocks**. Granite is a hard rock used to make buildings. Some rocks, like limestone, can be soft. Limestone was formed by dead ocean plants and animals. Chalk is a kind of limestone.

Lava rock comes from volcanoes. Pumice is a kind of lava rock. It is very light. Some pumice rocks can even float in water!

Coal is a rock that can be burned. It is used for heat.

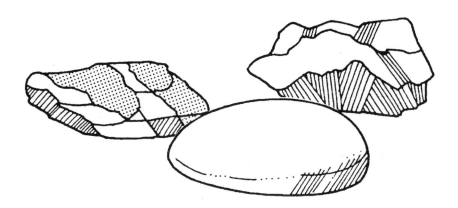

Complete the sentences below.

1. A rock used to make buildings is _____.

2. A rock that was formed by dead ocean plants and animals is

_____.

3. A rock that comes from volcanoes is _____.

4. A rock that can float in water is _____.

5. A rock that can be burned for heat is _____.

How Can You Group Rocks?

There are many kinds of rocks. Scientists often put rocks in groups to learn more about them. You can be a scientist in this activity.

You will need

⭐ 10 small rocks, some light colored, some dark

1. Bring some rocks to school.

2. Think about how the rocks are alike or different.

3. Put the rocks into groups.

4. Give each group a name.

📦 Answer the questions.

1. Did you group rocks by size? _____

2. Did you group rocks by color? _____

3. How else can you group rocks? _____

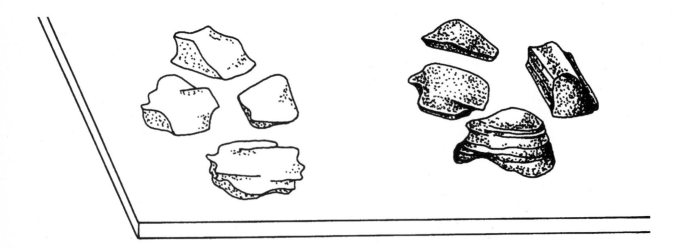

Rocks Change

You are learning about rocks. Rocks can be changed by wind, water, and plants. In this activity, you will observe rocks. You will tell how they are used and changed in your neighborhood.

1. In your neighborhood, look for rocks and for things made from rocks.

2. Think about these questions about each thing:
   a. What kind of material is it?
   b. How is it used?
   c. If it is changing, explain how and why.

Complete the chart. The first row is done for you.

Materials	How It Is Used	How It Is Changing	Causes of Changes
Example: cement	sidewalk	cracks	weeds and/or grass

Abrasion Changes Rocks

The land is always changing. One force that changes land is **abrasion**. Abrasion happens when one object rubs against another. Little pieces of the objects break off, and the objects are worn down.

When rocks rub against each other, the rocks get smaller. Tiny bits of them are worn away because of the abrasion. Sharp edges of them might get rounded. When rocks rub against each other in a stream, the rocks change in size and shape. When sand blows against rock, both the sand and the rock can be changed.

Complete the following exercises.

1. Draw a picture to show how this rock would change if other rocks rubbed against it for a long time.

2. Draw a picture to show how this rock would change if sand blew against it for a long time.

Water Changes the Land

Wherever there is water, the land around it is changed. You can see this if you look at a riverbank or an ocean shore. When the water moves over the land, it **erodes** the land, or wears it away.

Rain can erode land, too. When there is a lot of rain, an area can flood. The water in a flood washes away signs, cars, and even houses and roads.

Draw before-and-after pictures. Show how water changed something that you have seen.

1. Before	2. After

Water Changes Rocks

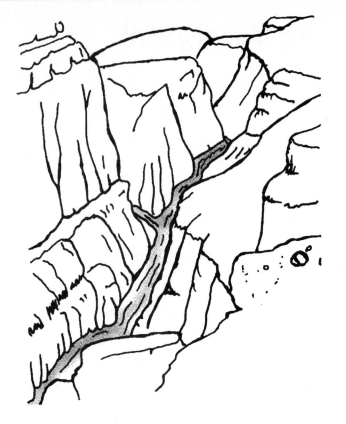

It took many years for the Grand Canyon to be formed. The water of the Colorado River washed over the rock and began to wear it away. This formed the walls of the canyon. Wind, rain, and melting snow caused more rock to wear away.

 Draw a picture of another kind of land that is formed by the movement of wind or water.

Our Changing Earth

Wind and water can change the Earth.

Look at the pictures below. Answer the questions. Then, color the pictures.

1. Which picture shows change by wind? _____

2. Which picture shows change by water? _____

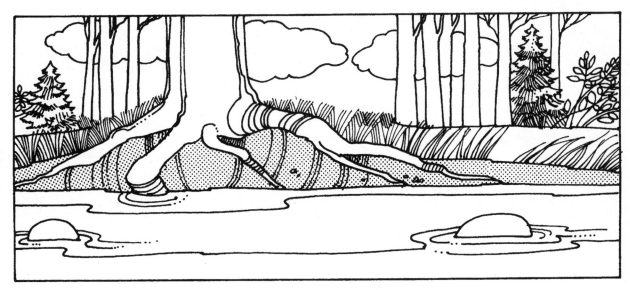

What's in Soil?

There are many things in **soil**. Look at soil around your school. Can you find these things? Give yourself a point for each thing you find.

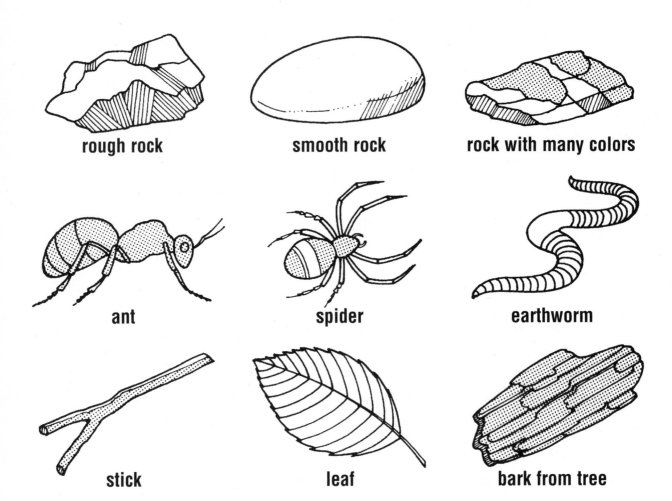

rough rock   smooth rock   rock with many colors

ant   spider   earthworm

stick   leaf   bark from tree

📦 **Keep score here.**

How Are Soils Different?

Soils are different in many ways. Study soils carefully in this activity.

You will need
- ⭐ sand
- ⭐ potting soil
- ⭐ samples of different kinds of soil from outside
- ⭐ hand lens
- ⭐ paper plates

1. Get some potting soil. Look at it with a hand lens.

2. Look at some sand.

3. Look at other different kinds of soil.

4. Write about what you see.

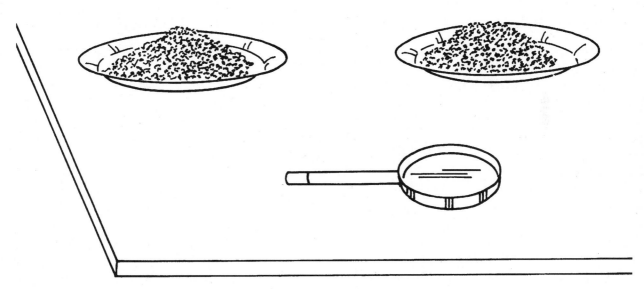

🔲 **Answer these questions on another sheet of paper.**

1. What is in each soil?

2. How are the soils different?

Layers of Rock

A **fossil** is the print or hardened shape of a plant or
an animal. Fossils are found in **rock layers**.
These layers of rock were once soil. Plants and
animals that died became buried in the soil.
Over many years, because of the pressure
of all the other soil above it, the soil
became rock. New layers of rock
keep forming over older layers.

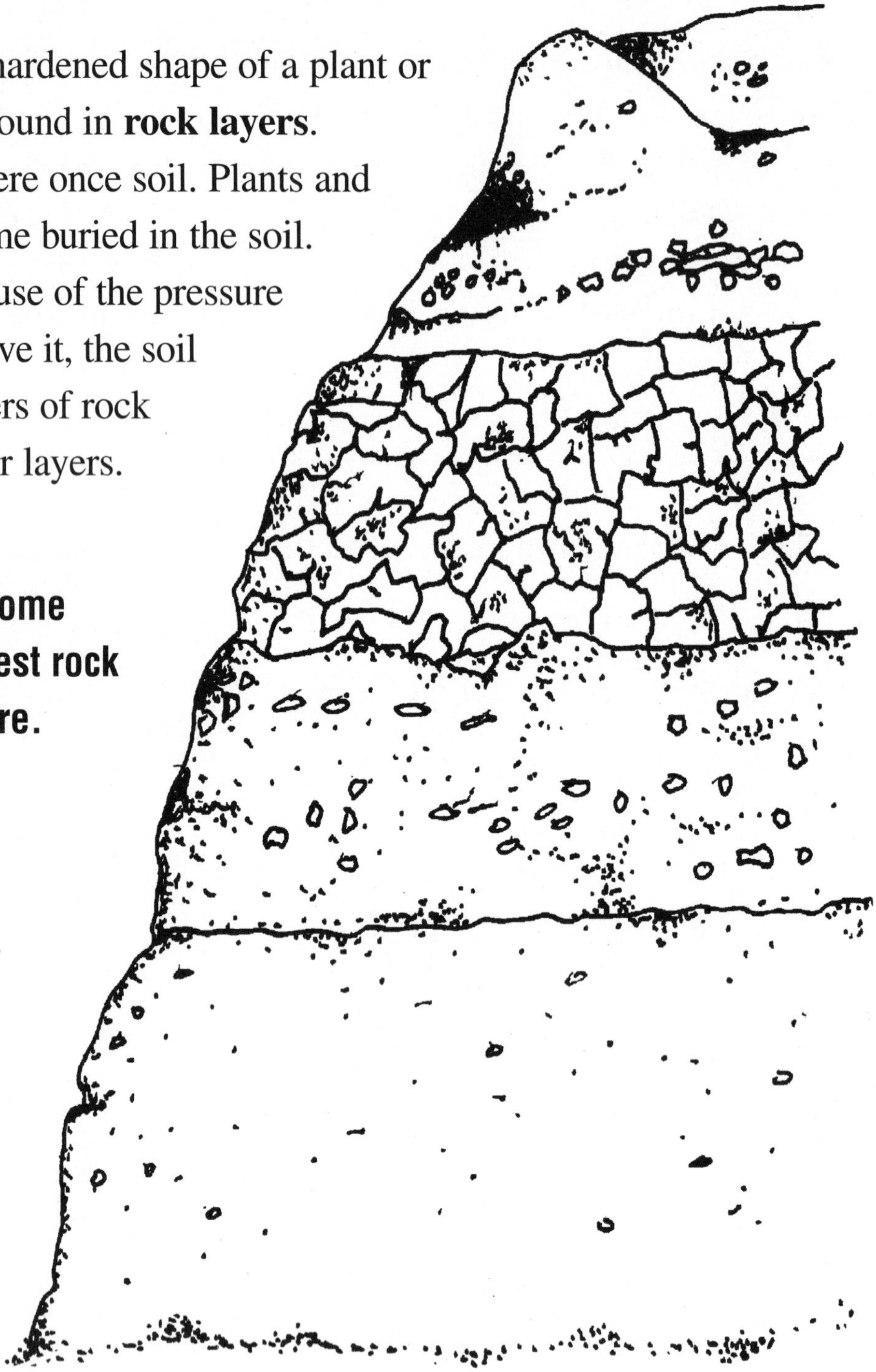

**Draw and color some
fossils in the oldest rock
layer in the picture.**

Fascinating Fossils

Since different rock layers form at different times, the fossils found in the layers are different, too. This helps scientists know when certain plants and animals lived. For example, fossils of starfish were found in deeper layers of rock than fossils of dinosaurs. Which animal lived first?

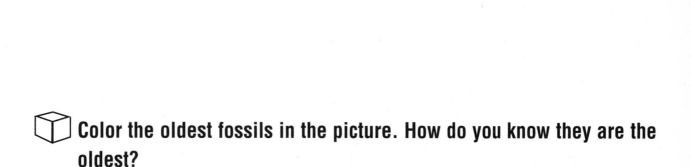

Color the oldest fossils in the picture. How do you know they are the oldest?

_____

_____

Fossils and Footprints

Scientists who study fossils are called **paleontologists**. Paleontologists have learned about plants and animals that lived on the Earth long before people were alive. How could they find out what happened long ago if no person was there to see it?

Paleontologists can tell some things about the way life was millions of years ago by observing fossils. Dinosaur fossils show the size of dinosaurs, what they ate, and how they moved. When different fossils are found together, they can even tell about an event that may have taken place long ago.

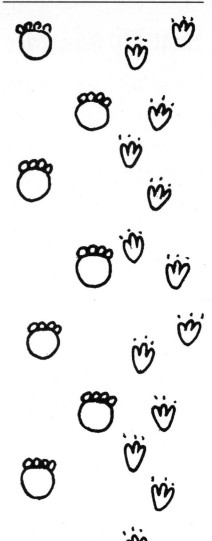

Look at these fossil footprints left by two dinosaurs. Study them carefully. What do they tell you?

_____

_____

_____

_____

_____

What Did Dinosaurs Look Like?

Dinosaurs were **reptiles** that lived on the Earth millions of years ago. You have probably seen colored pictures of dinosaurs. Most artists paint them brown, gray, or green. But no one really knows what color dinosaurs were. We do know about their skin because fossils of dinosaur skin have been found.

Dinosaur skin helped dinosaurs live in their environments. Some dinosaur skin may have been brightly colored. The bright skin could look scary to an enemy. It could also attract other dinosaurs.

Color these dinosaurs to show the way you think they might have looked.

What Happened to the Dinosaurs?

No dinosaurs live on the Earth today. They are **extinct**. That means that they don't exist now. There will never be any more of them.

Some scientists think that the dinosaurs died out from diseases. Others think that the Earth was hit by an asteroid from space. Others believe that volcanoes erupted. If those last two things happened, the air would be filled with dust. The light of the Sun would be blocked. That would have changed the weather. If dinosaurs or the things they ate couldn't live in the new weather, the dinosaurs would die out.

No one knows for sure why the dinosaurs became extinct. What do you think? Write your ideas.

_____

_____

_____

_____

_____

_____

_____

_____

The Water Cycle

Water changes in form all the time. We see liquid water in rivers, lakes, and oceans. Some of that water **evaporates** because of the wind and heat of the Sun. It changes into **water vapor**. When the water vapor **condenses**, it forms a cloud. When the droplets in the cloud become too heavy, they fall as rain. The same thing happens over and over. This is called the **water cycle**.

Add labels to this picture of the water cycle. Use the words in the box.

cloud	evaporate	ocean	rain	Sun

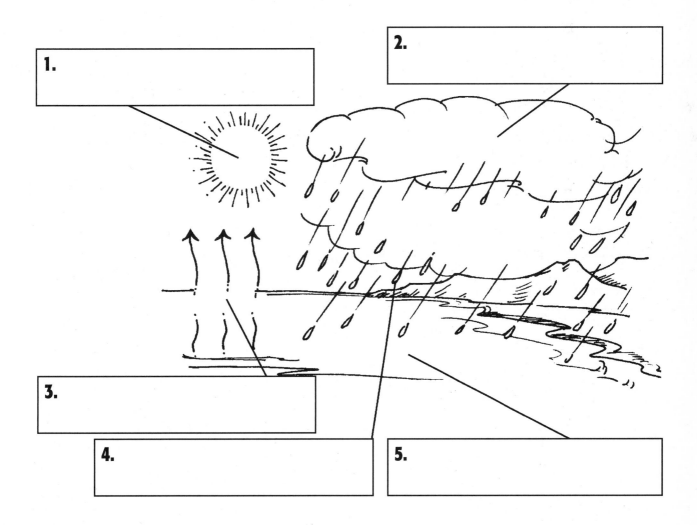

1.

2.

3.

4.

5.

Water Vapor

Water that is in the air is called **water vapor**. Where is water going into the air?

 To show where, draw an arrow like this. ⬆

What Happens to Water?

Water can change into a gas called water vapor. Heat can help the water change. See how water changes in this activity.

You will need
- ✭ 5 jars (without lids) or plastic cups
- ✭ masking tape
- ✭ water

1. Fill the jars with the same amount of water.

2. Use tape to mark the water level.

3. Put the jars in different places around the room.

4. Look at the jars in 2 or 3 days.

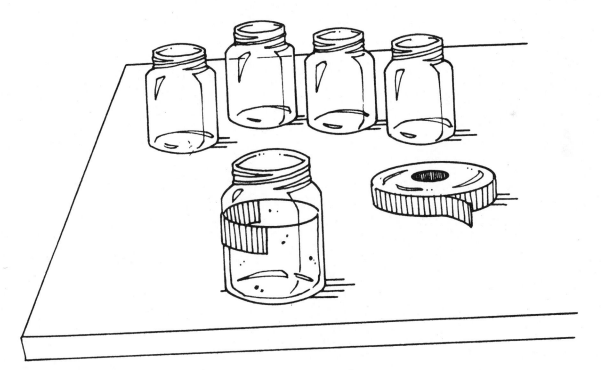

GO ON TO THE NEXT PAGE ☞

What Happens to Water?, p. 2

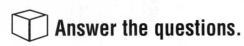 **Answer the questions.**

1. Did the level of the water change in any of the jars?

_____

_____

2. Did the water change by the same amount in every jar?

_____

_____

3. Tell why the level of the water changed.

_____

_____

_____

4. Where did the water go?

_____

_____

_____

Taking Water Out of the Air

Putting water into the air is something you have done often. For example, when you wash your hair, the water doesn't stay on your hair. It **evaporates**. But have you ever taken the water out of the air? Here is a way to change water vapor to liquid water.

You will need

- ⭐ empty can
- ⭐ water
- ⭐ 3 ice cubes
- ⭐ spoon
- ⭐ paper towel
- ⭐ food coloring

1. Fill the can halfway with cold water. Put in three drops of food coloring and stir. What color is the water? _____

2. Add the ice cubes. Wipe the outside of the can with the paper towel. Be sure the can is dry. Wait a few minutes.

Answer these questions.

1. What forms on the outside of the can? _____

2. What color are the drops? _____

3. Did they come from inside the can? _____

4. How do you know? _____

_____

The drops came from water vapor in the air. When water vapor is cooled, it collects into water droplets.

How Does Wind Change Water?

Water can change into a gas called water vapor. Heat and wind can help the water change. You will see how in this activity.

You will need

⭐ 2 small towels that are alike   ⭐ water

Note: Do this experiment on a sunny, windy day.

1. Wet each towel.

2. Hang one towel in a bathroom.

3. Hang one towel outside.

4. Look at the towels in two hours.

Answer these questions on another sheet of paper.

1. How did the towel in the bathroom feel?

2. How did the towel outside feel?

3. What helped one towel dry faster than the other?

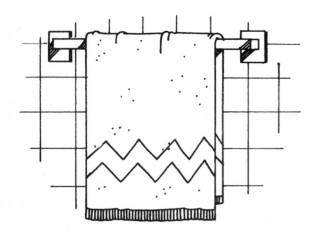

Does Air Take Up Space?

You know that air is matter. But does air take up space? Find out in this activity.

You will need
- ⭐ plastic drinking glass
- ⭐ aquarium tank or clear plastic shoe box
- ⭐ water

1. Turn a glass upside down.

2. Put the glass in water. Do not tilt it.

3. Hold the glass on the bottom of the tank.

4. Lift one side of the glass. Watch what happens.

Answer these questions on another sheet of paper.

1. What happened when you lifted one side of the glass?

2. Why did the air move?

3. Does the air take up space?

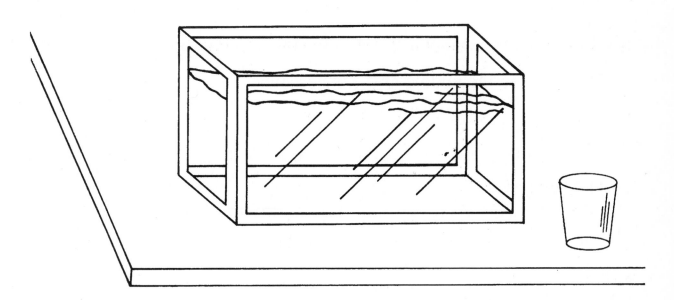

How Can You Weigh Air?

Does air weigh anything? Try this activity to find out.

You will need

★ 2 balloons ★ meter stick ★ 3 pieces of string ★ pin

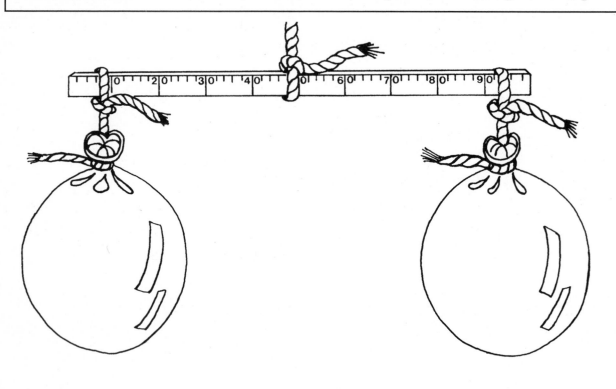

1. Blow up a balloon. Tie it with string to one end of a meter stick.

2. Blow up another balloon. Tie it to the other end of the stick.

3. Tie a string to the middle of the meter stick.

4. Hold the meter stick by the middle string.

5. Ask an adult to make a small hole near the knot of one balloon. Watch what happens.

Answer these questions on another sheet of paper.

1. What happened to the balloon with a hole?

2. Which side is heavier? Why?

Air and Weather

Air has a lot to do with the **weather**.

📦 **Cut out the sentences at the bottom of the page. Paste each one under the correct picture.**

✂

It is a wet day.	The air feels warm.
The wind is blowing.	The air feels cool.
It is not windy.	It is a dry day.

Name _____ Date _____

The Wind

The **wind** is another important part of the weather. What do you know about the wind?

□ **What things can the wind move? Take a walk on a windy day. List the things you see that are moved by the wind.**

1. _____   5. _____

2. _____   6. _____

3. _____   7. _____

4. _____   8. _____

□ **Sometimes the wind does useful things. Sometimes the wind does things that people don't like. What are some of these things? Write your answers in this chart.**

Ways That Wind Helps People	Ways That Wind Bothers People

What Kinds of Clouds Do You See?

Have you ever looked at the sky? Have you seen the **clouds** go rolling by? Clouds are another important part of the weather. There are many kinds and shapes of clouds. You will watch the clouds in this activity.

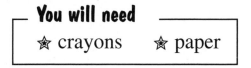

You will need

☆ crayons   ☆ paper

1. Look out the window. See what the clouds look like.

2. Draw a picture of the clouds.

3. Do this each day for one week. On each picture, write the name of the day.

4. In the chart, write what the weather was like for each day.

GO ON TO THE NEXT PAGE ☞

What Kinds of Clouds Do You See?, p. 2

⬜ **Complete the chart.**

	Monday	**Tuesday**	**Wednesday**	**Thursday**	**Friday**
Kind of Weather					

⬜ **Answer the questions.**

1. Were the clouds the same each day?

_____

2. What was the weather like? Was the weather the same each day?

_____

_____

3. How do clouds tell us about the weather?

_____

_____

_____

Clouds and Weather

📦 **Cut out the pictures at the bottom of the page. Paste each one in the correct box. Color the pictures.**

1. What are the clouds like here?

_____

3. What are the clouds like here?

_____

2. What is the weather like here?

_____

4. What is the weather like here?

_____

A Weather Puzzle

 **Use the picture clues to fill in the puzzle.**

1.

2.

3.

4.

5.

6.

What Will the Weather Be?

Can you predict the weather? Try this activity to find out.

You will need

☆ construction paper   ☆ crayons   ☆ scissors   ☆ thumbtacks

1. Draw pictures that show different kinds of weather. (sunny, cloudy, windy, rainy, snowy)

2. Today, guess what you think the weather will be like tomorrow. Put a picture of it on the chart. Make the weather chart for five days of the week.

3. Tomorrow, put another picture under the first one to show what the weather really was like.

4. Do this each day for one week. How many times were you right?

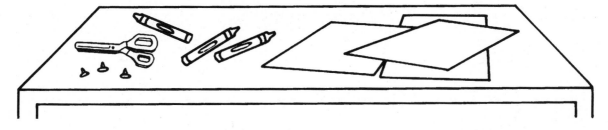

GO ON TO THE NEXT PAGE ☞

What Will the Weather Be?, p. 2

◻ **Complete the chart.**

	Monday	Tuesday	Wednesday	Thursday	Friday
I Think					
What the Weather Is					

◻ **Answer the questions.**

1. Did the weather change?

_____

2. Did you make good guesses?

_____

3. Tell how you know what guesses to make.

_____

_____

Dressing for the Weather

How would you dress for the weather?

▢ **Draw lines to match the clothes with the weather.**

1.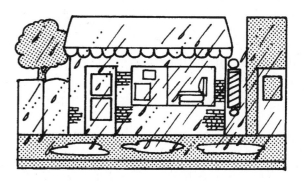

2.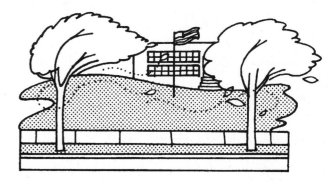

3.

4.

Thunderstorm Safety

**Read these rules with your family. Then, quiz each other. For example, ask, "What would you do if you were on the phone when a thunderstorm started?"**

Thunderstorm Safety Rules

1. Stay indoors.

2. Stay away from open windows.

3. Do not talk on the phone.

4. If you cannot get indoors, do not go under a tall tree. Try to get into thick woods.

5. Stay away from metal objects.

6. Get out of and away from water.

7. If you are in an open area, get down on your knees. Put your hands on your knees. Tuck your head.

Write a story about a thunderstorm. Pretend you are out in the open. Tell how you can be safe during the thunderstorm.

Earth and Sun

You have probably noticed that the shadow of a tree moves during the day. It seems to move from one side of the tree to the other. The shadow moves because the Earth rotates once each day. To us, it looks as if the Sun is moving. Sometimes we even talk about the Sun going up or coming down. But it is really the Earth that moves. As it moves, the shadows on the Earth change.

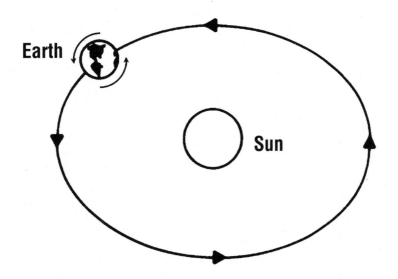

Write a sentence telling why outdoor shadows move during the day. Then, color the Earth and the Sun.

_____

_____

_____

_____

_____

_____

What Makes a Shadow?

If you look carefully, you can see **shadows** almost everywhere. Any object that blocks light makes a shadow. An outdoor shadow is made when an object blocks the light from the Sun. Indoors, light may be coming from a lamp. If there is no light, there won't be a shadow. The object that makes the shadow is always between the source of light and the shadow.

Draw shadows for the objects in the picture.

Shapes of Shadows

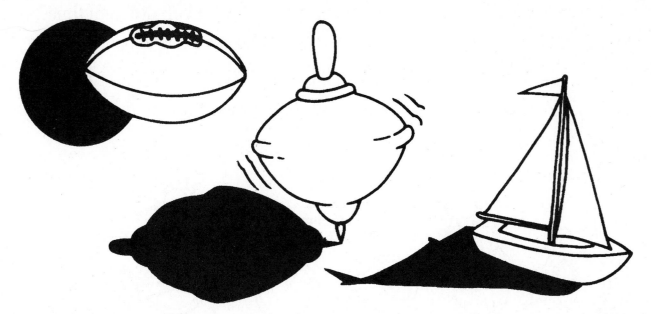

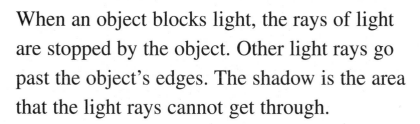

Look at shadows around you. Is the shadow of a pencil the same shape as the pencil? Is the shadow of a bicycle the same shape as the bicycle? You will see that shadows have a shape that is like the object that makes them. Why do you think this is so?

When an object blocks light, the rays of light are stopped by the object. Other light rays go past the object's edges. The shadow is the area that the light rays cannot get through.

 **Color the toys that have the correct shadows.**

Outdoor Shadows

If you went outdoors and measured the same shadow at two different times, you would find that the shadow changes size. Why does this happen?

The size and position of a shadow change because the position of the Sun changes. Look at where the Sun is in these pictures. Look at the size and position of the shadows.

You can see that the size and position of the shadow changed as the Earth moved.

⬜ **In these three boxes, draw your own changing shadows.**

1.	2.	3.

Make a Book of the Planets

1. Cut both pages on the dotted lines.

2. Fold each piece in half so the picture is on the left. Tape the ends.

3. Put the pages together like this.

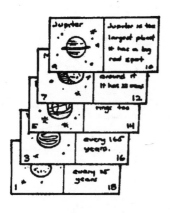

4. Staple here.

Pluto revolves around the Sun every 248 years. 18

Neptune revolves around the Sun every 165 years. 16

Mercury 1

Venus 3

Mini-Book Our Solar System 2

Mercury is the planet closest to the Sun.

This book belongs to 19

Pluto 17

GO ON TO THE NEXT PAGE ☞

Make a Book of the Planets, p. 2

Uranus has moons and rings, too.

14

Saturn has many, many rings around it. It has 23 moons!

12

Jupiter is the largest planet. It has a big red spot.

10

Earth

5

Mars

7

Jupiter

9

Spacecraft have landed on Venus and sent pictures back to Earth.

4

We live on the Earth. It has water and many living things.

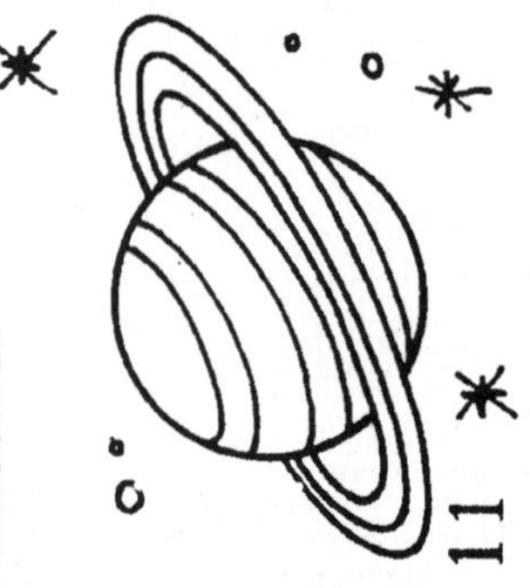

6

Mars is called the "Red Planet." It has red soil.

8

Neptune

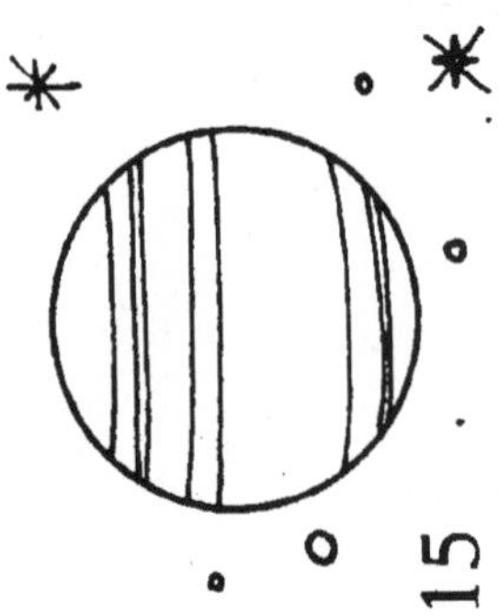

15

Uranus

13°

Saturn

11

See the Planets!

Imagine that you are an astronaut. You are riding in a space shuttle. You are about to go by the Sun. Next, you will go by each of the planets. List the names of the planets you go by in order below.

Mercury Venus Earth Mars Jupiter Saturn Uranus Neptune Pluto

1. <u>Sun</u>

2. _____

3. _____

4. _____

5. _____

6. _____

7. _____

8. _____

9. _____

10. _____

Earth, Mars, and Jupiter

Earth, Mars, and Jupiter are alike in some ways. They are different in other ways. Read about these planets in a science book.

Read each statement in the chart below. If the statement is true for Earth, put an X on the line under Earth. If it is true for Mars, put an X on the line under Mars. If it is true for Jupiter, put an X on the line under Jupiter. A statement may be true for more than one planet.

	Earth	Mars	Jupiter
1. It travels around the Sun.			
2. It has two moons.			
3. Of the three planets, it gets the most energy from the Sun.			
4. It has the longest orbit of the three planets.			
5. It has the shortest orbit of the three planets.			
6. It has iron in its soil.			
7. It has ice caps.			
8. It has the Giant Red Spot.			
9. It has a small ring around it.			
10. It has life on it.			
11. It is called the "Red Planet."			

Space Station!

Can people live in outer space? Some people have already. In 1998, parts of the new International Space Station were launched into space. More parts are being built. It is planned to be complete by 2006. It will orbit 200 miles above Earth.

Who will live on the Space Station? Now, the space station has a crew of only three to six people. These astronauts may be from the United States, Russia, Japan, and European countries. These are the main nations building the space station.

What does the crew do? They study life in space. They do experiments. Later, they may repair satellites. Their food supplies come from space shuttles that fly to the space station. The crew works on the space station for six months and then returns to Earth. They hope to show how well people can live in space.

Pretend that you live on the space station. What would your job be? What would your daily life be like? Write about it. Use another sheet of paper.

Light for the Moon and Earth

The Sun gives light to the Moon
and the Earth.

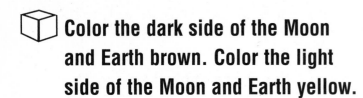 **Color the dark side of the Moon
and Earth brown. Color the light
side of the Moon and Earth yellow.**

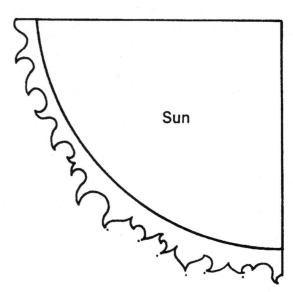

Sun

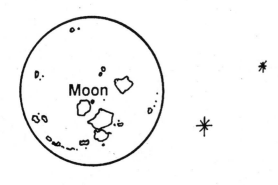

Moon

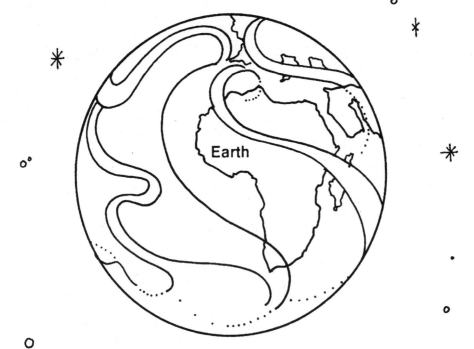

Earth

Everything Moves in Space

Everything in space is always moving.

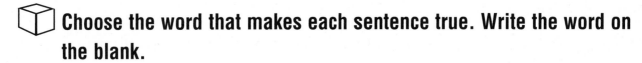 **Choose the word that makes each sentence true. Write the word on the blank.**

| revolves | rotate | Sun | light | planets |

1. The Earth and Moon turn, or _____.

2. The Moon _____ around the Earth.

3. We see the Moon because of _____ from the Sun.

4. Both the Earth and Moon revolve around the _____.

5. The _____ all move in space.

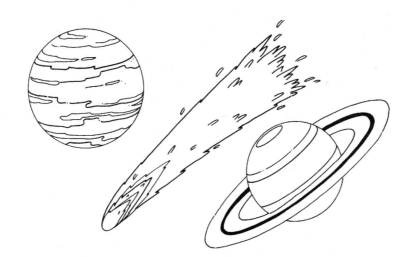

Star Gazing

In ancient times, people knew the **stars** well. Travelers could tell direction by looking at the stars.

A **constellation** is a group of stars that has a pattern. A constellation looks like a picture. Find a book on constellations. Go outside on a clear night. It is best to view the sky by lying on your back with your head toward the north and your feet toward the south.

Try to locate the following constellations: the Big Dipper, Leo, Orion, Canis Major, Taurus, Cancer, and Cassiopeia the Queen. See how many more you know.

Write the names of these constellations.

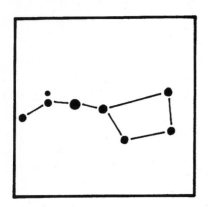 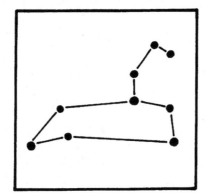 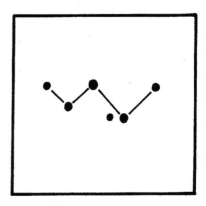

1. _____ 2. _____ 3. _____

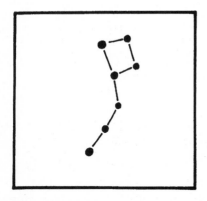 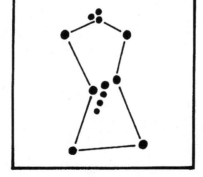

4. _____ 5. _____

Unit 3: Life Science

BACKGROUND INFORMATION

Living and Nonliving Things

Living things carry on activities that nonliving things do not. These life processes define a living thing. All living things grow, or increase in size and the amount of matter they contain. All living things can reproduce, or make more of the same kind of organism. Living things consume energy, change it, and excrete, or give off, waste. Living things react to stimuli and to changes in the environment.

Nonliving things may carry on some of these activities, but because they do not carry on all of these activities, they are not living. Students may be confused about what is living and what is not. Water seems to move, change, and appear alive. A flame will flicker and grow. Even scientists disagree about certain things, such as viruses. Distinguishing between living and nonliving things can be difficult, but students can follow the guidelines above to grasp the concept.

Life Cycles

All living things go through life cycles. From single-celled organisms to the largest animals, these life cycles include growth, change, consumption of food and water, use of energy, reproduction, and death. Reproduction varies among life forms. Plants reproduce by seeds or spores. Animals may lay eggs or give birth to live young. Some offspring resemble the parents and others do not. Some animals, such as frogs, undergo metamorphosis, or a complete change, during their lifetimes. The successful reproduction of a species is important to that population's continued growth or stability.

Adaptations to Environment

For living things to remain alive, they must respond to changes or conditions in their habitat or environment. Environments include all the conditions in which a living thing exists. This includes the food the organism needs, water, soil, air, temperature, and climate. Common environments are deserts, grasslands, oceans, and forests. Each of these larger environments contains many smaller environments. There are ponds and swamps in the forest. Deserts can be hot or cold. The living and nonliving things in each environment interact with each other. When environments are threatened or changed in drastic ways, the living things in the environment are also threatened.

The Human Factor

Organisms need to adapt to and change with the changes in their environment to survive. If they cannot adapt, they will not survive. Organisms adapt through physical changes that help them live in their particular habitats and through habits, such as migration, that help them survive. Although many events can disrupt a community and its balance, humans have had the greatest impact upon the Earth's environment. Humans need not only food and energy but also power and space for settlement. Humans create wastes that are not natural to the environment. This environmental pollution is an important concern for everyone. If it is not controlled, the balance of nature is disrupted, organisms die, and those that depend upon the dead organisms may die. It is crucial for humans to find ways to live without creating such disturbances in the environment.

Plant Classification

The plant kingdom contains about 450,000 different kinds of plants, which are each classified into several divisions. The four main classifications for plants are: algae (almost all live in water; from microscopic single-celled plants to seaweed); bryophyta (mosses and liverworts; live in moist places; produce spores); pteridophyta (ferns, clubmosses, horsetails; no flowers); and permatophyta (largest group, with over 350,000 species; reproduce by seeds).

Spermatophytes are divided into two categories, the gymnosperms and the angiosperms. Gymnosperms, or "naked seed" plants, have seeds in cones, like pinecones from conifer trees. The angiosperms, or "covered seed" plants, include all of the flowering plants.

Flowering plants are the most numerous type of plant on Earth. They are further classified into groups. Some of the common groups of flowering plants are: grass family (corn, barley, rice, wheat); lily family (violets, hyacinths, tulips, onions, asparagus); palm family (coconut, date); rose family (strawberries, peaches, cherries, apples, and other fruits); legume family (peas, beans, peanuts); beech family; and composite family (sunflowers and others with flowers that are actually many small flowers).

Plants are also classified as vascular and nonvascular. Vascular plants have tubes that bring the liquids the plants need from their environment up through the stalk. The tubes also help to support the plants. Nonvascular plants, such as mosses, do not have tubes. They are shorter because they must remain close to their source of moisture. They get the water and nutrients they need through their root systems.

Photosynthesis
Most plants are green. The reason that green plants are green is because they contain chlorophyll, most of which is in the leaves. There are some plants that contain chlorophyll but whose leaves are not green. This is because the chlorophyll has been masked by other pigmentation in the plant. Chlorophyll is necessary for the making of food, but the chlorophyll itself is not used in the food that is made.

Photosynthesis depends on light. A plant that is deprived of light loses its chlorophyll (and its ability to make food) and eventually will die. Plants take in the energy from the sun and carbon, oxygen, and hydrogen from the air and water. They change these raw materials into carbohydrates and oxygen. The carbohydrates are used and stored in the plants for food. The oxygen is released into the air and water where the plants live. In this way, plants constantly replenish the Earth's oxygen supply.

Reproduction
Plants reproduce from seeds in flowers, from seeds in cones, or from spores. The seeds form after fertilization of their egg cells by male cells from pollen grains. Pollen can be carried to the egg cells by bees or other insects, by the wind, or by animals.

Seeds contain tiny plants called embryos around which a store of food is packed. In some seeds, such as bean seeds, the food is stored inside the embryo. Seeds are spread by animals and the wind. When the seeds in a cone are ripe, the cone will open, and the seeds will float to the ground or be carried by the wind. Some seeds have tiny parachutes to help them drift. A seed needs moisture, warmth, and carbon dioxide to begin growing into a new plant. If conditions are not right for germination, some seeds can remain in a resting state for hundreds of years.

Life Cycle
The life cycle of a seed plant begins with an embryo. An embryo is an undeveloped living thing that comes from a fertilized egg. The eggs in a flowering plant are called ovules. When the ovules are fertilized, they begin to grow. A seed is a complete embryo plant surrounded by the food it needs to grow and protected by a coating. When the seed is planted, or lands on the ground, it begins to sprout. It grows into a seedling, then an adult plant that develops flowers in which new seeds grow.

Animal Classification
The animal kingdom can be classified into two large groups: the vertebrates (those with backbones) and the invertebrates (those without backbones). The backbone

supports the body and provides flexibility. The spinal cord extends from the brain through the backbone, or spine. Individual nerves branch out from the spinal cord to different parts of the body. Messages from the brain are sent throughout the body through the spinal cord.

Some animals without backbones are sponges, jellyfish, clams, worms, insects, and spiders. Some of these animals have networks of nerves throughout their bodies with no central nerve cords. Many, like insects, have hard exoskeletons that protect their bodies and give them shape.

Animals are further categorized into six groups:

- Mammals are identified as animals that have hair or fur, feed milk to their young, and are warm-blooded. Warm-blooded animals are able to withstand a wide variety of temperatures and still keep their bodies warm, so they are found almost everywhere. Mammals are vertebrates and breathe through their lungs. Mammals' eggs are fertilized internally, and the babies are born alive. Mammals are capable of learning and have highly developed brains. Some mammals are carnivores (such as lions and dogs) and eat only animals, or meat; some are herbivores (such as rabbits and giraffes) and eat only plants; and some are omnivores (such as bears and skunks) and eat both animals and plants.

- Amphibians are animals that live both on land and in water. They are cold-blooded animals, most with smooth, wet skin. Most lay eggs in the water and move onto the land as they get older. Amphibians undergo a metamorphosis in which their form changes completely. For example, frogs lay their eggs in the water. The eggs grow into tadpoles with heads, gills, and no legs. Then, they develop two legs. Later, they develop two more legs and lungs, and their tails begin to disappear. Finally, they have four fully grown legs, no tails, and no gills, and they leave the water to live on land. Most amphibians are herbivores when they are born and carnivores when they become adults living on land. Amphibians can breathe through their skin as well as with their lungs. Most amphibians with legs have webbed feet.

- Reptiles are scaly-skinned, cold-blooded animals. Their body temperatures vary with the temperature of the air around them. Reptiles get energy from the warmth of the Sun. They get sluggish when they are cold. Their skin feels dry and hard. Some reptiles have four legs, and some do not have any legs. Some reptiles bear live young, but most lay eggs. Baby reptiles look much like their parents and can care for themselves from birth. Although many reptiles can swim, they do not breathe under water. They breathe air with their lungs. Reptiles live in forests, jungles, and deserts.

- Birds are the only creatures with feathers. They are warm-blooded vertebrates. Most birds have hollow bones and powerful wing muscles that enable them to fly. Some, such as the ostrich, do not fly. Birds' eggs are fertilized in the body, a protective shell is formed, and the bird lays the eggs. Birds care for their young until they are able to fly and get their own food.

- Fish are fitted to their environment because of their gills, which enable them to absorb oxygen from the water. They use their fins and tails to move and are covered with scales. Fish reproduce by external fertilization; the female lays the eggs (spawns) and the male deposits sperm over the eggs. Fish are divided into three groups: jawless fish, cartilage fish, and bony fish. Fish are cold-blooded animals. Their bodies are the temperature of the water in which they live.

- Arthropods are animals without backbones. They have jointed legs, a segmented body, and an exoskeleton. Insects make up the majority of arthropods. Insects have three body parts: the head, the thorax, and the abdomen. The eyes, antennas, and mouths are on the head. Insects have six legs. Some have wings. All insects have a tough exoskeleton. This protects the insect's organs but must be shed as the insect grows. Insects undergo either a complete or an incomplete metamorphosis as they develop from egg to maturity. A complete metamorphosis includes four stages: the egg, the larva, the pupa, and the adult. The incomplete metamorphosis includes an egg stage, a nymph stage, and the adult stage.

Animals and Their Environments

Animals live in almost every type of environment on Earth. Each kind of animal has become well suited to its environment through generations of adaptation. Animals that are not suited to the environment, or that are poorly adapted, do not survive. The animals that are most fit for their environments continue to reproduce and make others like themselves. Most animals are suited to either land or water life. An obvious adaptation for fish is the gills that allow them to breathe in the water. Lungs allow land animals to breathe in air.

Every part of an animal helps it to live in its particular environment. Some animals are colored in ways that help them blend in to their environments. They are camouflaged to protect them from their enemies. Other animals are brightly colored to attract mates and help them with the continuation of their species. Animals' mouths and teeth are adapted to the types of food that they eat. Meat-eating animals have sharp teeth for tearing and ripping their prey, and other teeth for chewing the meat. Animals that eat leaves and grasses have large flat teeth for chewing.

The beaks and feet of different birds vary greatly. Some birds have thick, short beaks for cracking seeds. Others have long, slender beaks that they dip into flowers to reach nectar. The heron uses its long beak like tweezers to pluck fish from the water. Woodpeckers have beaks strong enough to hammer holes into trees as they look for insects. Eagles have strong, thick claws that enable them to grasp and carry their prey.

The webbed feet of ducks help them to swim. Some birds have feet that help them to climb, and others have feet that are best suited for perching.

Insects also have different types of mouth parts depending on their diets; some have chewing mouth parts to eat plants, and others have sucking mouth parts to get liquids.

Reproduction

Animals reproduce in different ways. Some lay eggs, and others give birth to live young. Some offspring look like their parents while others do not. Most reptiles, amphibians, fish, and insects lay eggs. The young of many of these animals can move about and find food for themselves soon after they hatch. Birds also lay eggs, but the adult birds remain with the eggs and care for the young until they can find their own food. Most mammals bear live young. The young are fed milk from the body. Mammals spend more time than other animals feeding, protecting, and teaching their young to survive on their own. Animals that give birth to live young have fewer offspring than those that do not tend to their young. The young of human beings require more care from their parents than any other animal.

Health

Health for children revolves around healthy foods, plenty of exercise, and good hygiene. As children grow, they should begin to recognize that they can make choices that will help them live healthy lives. They need to learn the connections between what they eat and the way they look and feel. They need to have the basic information that will help them to make good food choices. Children need to know that it is never too early to begin healthy habits in eating, exercise, and hygiene. The habits they form now will affect their lives for many years to come.

Nutrition

The body needs to receive certain nutrients in order to grow and to stay healthy. These nutrients are broken down into six types:

carbohydrates, protein, fat, vitamins, minerals, and water.

- Carbohydrates are sugars and starches. Sugars, such as fruits and honey, give the body quick energy while the starches, such as bread, cereal, and rice, give the body stored energy.

- Proteins come from foods such as milk, cheese, lean meat, fish, peas, and beans. They help the body to repair itself. Proteins are used by the body to build muscle and bone, and they give the body energy.

- Fat is important for energy, too, and it helps to keep the body warm, but if the body does not use the fats put into it, it will store the fat. Fats come from foods such as meat, milk, butter, oil, and nuts.

- Vitamins are important to the body in many ways. Vitamins help the other nutrients in a person's body work together. Lack of certain vitamins can cause serious illnesses. Vitamin A, for example, from foods such as broccoli, carrots, radishes, and liver, helps with eyesight. Vitamin B from green leafy vegetables, eggs, and milk, helps with growth and energy. Vitamin C from citrus fruits, cauliflower, strawberries, tomatoes, peppers, and broccoli, prevents sickness.

- Minerals necessary for growth are found in milk, vegetables, liver, seafood, and raisins. Calcium is a mineral that helps with strong bones, and iron is needed for healthy red blood.

- Water makes up most of the human body and helps to keep our temperature normal. It is healthy and recommended to drink several glasses of water each day.

Foods have long been divided into four basic food groups: meat, milk, vegetable-fruit, and bread-cereal. New discoveries have led to a change in the divisions so that in a food pyramid, fruits and vegetables are separated, and fats are included at the top of the pyramid. The recommended servings for each group have also changed over time. Eating the right amount of foods from each group each day gives one a balanced diet. Eating too many foods from one group or not enough of another can lead to deficiencies or weight problems. Although vitamin supplements can help with these deficiencies, vitamins are best absorbed in the body naturally through the digestion of the foods that contain them.

- The Bread-Cereal (Grain) Group contains foods made from grains such as wheat, corn, rice, oats, and barley. Six to eleven servings from this group each day give you carbohydrates, vitamins, and minerals.

- The Vegetable and Fruit Groups contain vitamins, minerals, and carbohydrates. Two to four servings of fruits and three to five servings of vegetables each day are recommended.

- The Meat Group includes chicken, fish, red meats, peas, nuts, and eggs. The meat group contains much of the protein we get from our diets, but it also includes fats. Two to three servings from the meat group each day are recommended.

- The Milk Group includes milk (whole and skim), butter, cheese, yogurt, and ice cream and gives us fat, vitamins, protein, and minerals that are important for strong bones and teeth. Two to three servings from the milk group each day are recommended.

- The Fats, Oils, and Sweets Group, including butter, oil, and margarine, should be used sparingly.

Hygiene

Keeping the body clean is an important part of staying healthy. Children need to know that when they wash, they are washing off viruses and bacteria, or germs, which can cause illness. Washing the hair and body regularly prevents bacteria from entering the skin through cuts and from getting into the mouth. Hands should always be washed after handling garbage or using the bathroom. Regular brushing and flossing can help keep teeth healthy.

Germs can also come from other people. Children should be discouraged from sharing straws, cups, or other utensils. They should be reminded always to cover their mouths when they sneeze or cough, and to use tissues frequently. Children also need to be reminded not to share combs or hats.

The Five Senses and the Nervous System

The human body collects information using the five senses: sight, smell, hearing, taste, and touch. The nervous system enables us to put all of our senses together so that messages are sent to the brain and we are able to act according to the information that the brain receives. The nervous system enables us to react. It controls all of the other systems in the body.

The major organ of the nervous system is the brain. Another part of the nervous system is a system of nerves that carry information to the brain. The third part of the nervous system is the sense organs. For example, the nose is the sense organ for the sense of smell. There are many nerve cells in the nose that take the information regarding odors to a main nerve called the olfactory nerve. The olfactory nerve carries the information to your brain. Your brain will then tell your body what to do with the information.

Safety

Children need to take part in ensuring their own safety. They need to be provided with the information necessary to stay safe as they do more and more on their own. Basic safety rules for water and thunderstorms are reviewed in this book. Children should also be aware of basic bicycle safety rules. Class discussions about these important safety rules should be conducted. Students should be encouraged to discuss why the rules are important and the consequences of not following the rules.

RELATED READING

- *About Amphibians: A Guide for Children* by Cathryn P. Sill (Peachtree, 2001).

- *About Reptiles: A Guide for Children* by Cathryn P. Sill (Peachtree, 1999).

- *Autumn Leaves* by Ken Robbins (Scholastic, 1998).

- *Bugs Are Insects* by Anne Rockwell (*Let's-Read-and-Find-Out Science Series*, HarperCollins, 2001).

- *Dandelions: Stars in the Grass* by Mia Posada (Carolrhoda, 2000).

- *Exercise and Your Health* and *Food and Your Health* by Jillian Powell (*Health Matters Series*, Raintree Steck-Vaughn, 1998).

- *How Your Body Works Series* by Carol Ballard (Raintree Steck-Vaughn, 1998).

- *Microhabitats Series* by Clare Oliver (Raintree Steck-Vaughn, 2002).

- *Ten Seeds* by Ruth Brown (Alfred A. Knopf, 2001).

Unit 3 Assessment

⬜ **Write your answers.**

1. Name a hot, dry habitat. _____

2. Name a warm, wet habitat. _____

3. Tell four things that living things need.

   a. _____ b. _____

   c. _____ d. _____

4. What does pollution do to a habitat?

   _____

   _____

⬜ **Draw a picture of a flower. Label its roots, stem, leaves, and flower.**

5. Write **a** on the part of the plant that makes food.

6. Write **b** on the part that carries food and water through the plant.

7. Write **c** on the part that carries water from the soil to the plant.

8. Write **d** on the part of the plant that makes seeds.

GO ON TO THE NEXT PAGE ☞

Unit 3 Assessment, p. 2

☐ **Complete the chart about animals. Some spaces are filled in for you.**

Kind of Animal	How It Looks or Feels	How It Moves (most often)	How It Gives Birth	Name an Animal
	has fur, soft			hamster
Reptile		slithers		
Amphibian			eggs in water	
	has scales			
Bird			eggs in nest	
		crawls		ant

☐ **Choose a sense you can use to learn about each thing. Draw a line from the sense to the thing.**

9. sight

10. smell

11. touch

12. hearing

13. taste

a. rose

b. bunny

c. ice cream

d. smoke

e. radio

Homes Are Habitats

A **habitat** is the natural home of a plant or animal. It is the place where a plant or an animal lives and grows on its own. Oceans, deserts, forests, and rain forests are habitats. Many plants and animals live in each of these habitats.

📦 **Draw a line from each animal to its habitat.**

1.

2.

3.

4.

What Do Animals Need?

A **garden** is a habitat. A habitat is a place where an animal or a plant lives. It has all the things in it that the living thing needs: food, water, air, and shelter.

In the garden, animals find leaves or other food they need to eat. When it rains, the water is trapped in the soil or on leaves. This is used by the animals. They can get the air they need above ground or below ground. The animals find shelter under rocks, leaves, or underground.

What are the four things an animal needs in its habitat? Write on the lines.

1. _____   2. _____

3. _____   4. _____

126

Earthworms

Many animals live in garden habitats. Some live above the ground. Some live below the ground. Worms are animals that live in gardens. Worms tunnel through the ground. The tunnels help air and water get into the soil. They give roots room to grow. Worms leave droppings that are good for plants. Plants help worms, too. Worms eat dead parts of plants as they tunnel through the soil.

Draw worms in these underground tunnels. Show what they are eating.

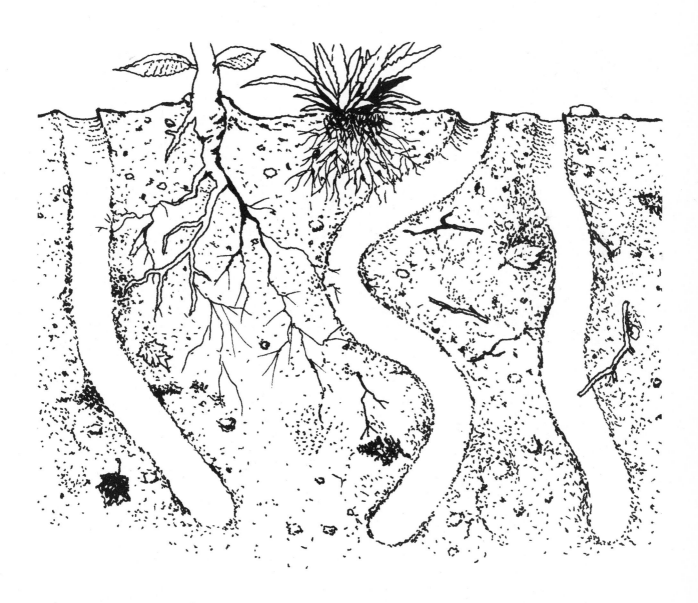

This Place Is Dry!

There is little water for plants in the **desert**. Desert plants store water in their stems. Then they can get the water they need, even when it doesn't rain for a long time.

The **cactus** plant grows in the desert. It has a thick skin that protects it from the hot weather. It also has sharp needles that keep some animals from eating it.

Find the cacti in the picture. Then, color their stems green and their needles brown.

This Place Is Wet!

This is Jane's plant. One day after she planted it, she saw drops of water on the side of the jar. "Where did this water come from?" Jane asked.

"This is what happens," said Jane's teacher. "The plants take up water from the soil. The plants give off some water into the air. Water also moves from the soil into the air. The lid on the jar keeps the air inside. Then, the Sun warms the air in the jar. And the water comes back out of the air in little drops. So the plants can use the same water over and over again."

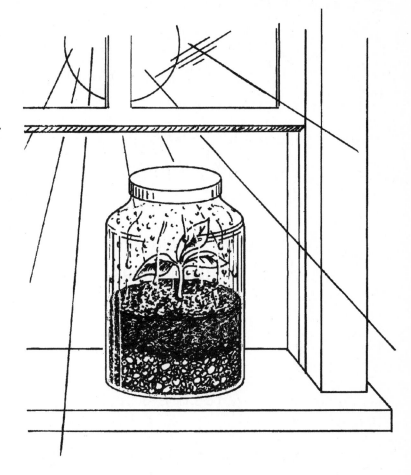

Where did the water on the side of the jar come from? Circle two things in the picture to show your answer. Then, write your answer below.

_____

_____

_____

_____

_____

Environments

The garden habitat is an **environment**. An environment is everything around a living thing. There are plants, animals, rocks, water, soil, and air in a garden environment.

Plants and animals interact with each other in their environments. **Interact** means to affect each other in different ways. For example, plants can be food for animals. Animals can carry the seeds of plants to other places.

Draw a picture of your environment. Show the living and nonliving things.

A Salty World

The water in oceans is salty. This water is called **salt water**. But water in lakes, ponds, rivers, and streams is not salty. It is called **fresh water**.

A change of habitat can harm a plant or animal. Sea plants and animals need the salt water of an ocean to live. They could not live in the fresh water of a lake or pond. And the plants and animals in a lake or pond could not live in the salty ocean.

Draw a picture of a water animal that could not live in fresh water.

Plants in the Garden

Plants are one of the things in a garden. Like other living things, plants need food, water, and air to live. Most plants have three parts: roots, stems, and leaves. These plant parts use the food, water, and air in different ways to keep the whole plant alive.

Draw a plant that you have seen. Draw and label the roots, stems, and leaves.

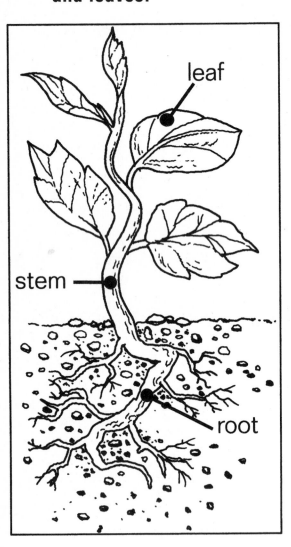

How Does Water Get Into a Plant?

You know that plants need water to live. But how does water get into a plant? Do this activity to find out.

You will need
- ☆ glass
- ☆ toothpicks
- ☆ red food coloring
- ☆ potato
- ☆ knife
- ☆ water

1. Put toothpicks into the sides of a potato.

2. Put some water in a glass. Mix red food coloring with the water.

3. Put the potato into this mixture.

4. Wait a few days. Have an adult cut the potato in half.

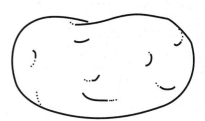

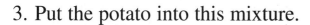 Answer the questions.

1. How did the potato change?

_____

_____

_____

2. Tell why the potato changed.

_____

_____

_____

How Does Water Travel Through a Plant?

Some plants have tiny **tubes** in them.
The tubes carry water through the
plants. See how in this activity.

You will need
- ⭐ glass jar
- ⭐ red food coloring
- ⭐ stalk of celery with leaves
- ⭐ magnifying glass
- ⭐ water
- ⭐ table knife

1. Mix food coloring in some water.

2. Put a stalk of celery into the water.

3. Wait a day. Look at the leaves.

4. Cut off a piece of the stalk.

 **Answer the questions.**

1. What happened to the leaves?

_____

_____

2. What did you see when you cut the stalk?

_____

_____

3. Tell how water travels to the leaves of a plant.

_____

_____

Roots

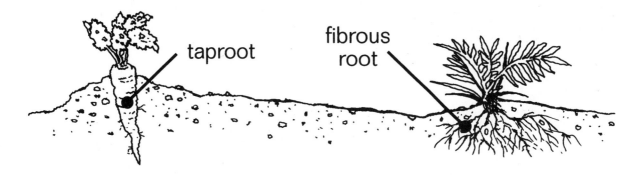

taproot

fibrous
root

Roots help a plant by holding it in the ground. Roots also take in water and nutrients from the soil. Nutrients help make plants healthy.

There are two kinds of roots. A **taproot** is long and thick. It can get water and nutrients that are deep in the soil. A carrot is a taproot. The other kind of root is a **fibrous root**. These roots are short and thin. They get water and nutrients that are near the top of the soil. Grass has fibrous roots.

Finish this chart. Use the words in the box.

short	long	thick	thin

taproot	fibrous roots

Stems

Stems are very important parts of plants. Stems carry the water and nutrients from the roots of plants to their leaves. Stems carry food to all parts of plants. Stems also hold plants up toward the Sun's light. Without light, plants would die.

▢ Draw ⬆ to show how water travels through this plant.

Leaves

Leaves grow in many shapes and sizes. Each kind of plant has its own kind of leaves. But leaves can be sorted into three main kinds.

Some trees have **broad leaves**. Broad leaves are wide. Maple and oak trees have broad leaves. Trees with broad leaves are called **deciduous trees**.

Some trees have **narrow leaves**. Just as their name says, they are narrow! Grasses have narrow leaves.

Some trees have **needle leaves**. They are narrow and pointed, like a needle. Fir and pine trees have needle leaves. Trees with needle leaves are called **evergreens**. Evergreens stay green all year.

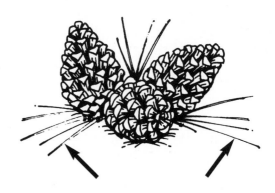

☐ **On another sheet of paper, draw some leaves. Write whether they are <u>broad</u>, <u>narrow</u>, or <u>needle</u> leaves. Color the leaves.**

Leaves at Work

Leaves help a plant by making food for it. The leaves use sunlight, water, and air to make the food. Then, the stem carries this food back through the rest of the plant. Without food, the plant could not grow flowers and seeds.

 Draw two things that are needed for this plant to make food for itself.

Seeds

Seeds are found in the flower of a plant. Seeds are many shapes and sizes. On the outside of a seed is a seed coat. The seed coat protects the seed. Inside the seed are the embryo and food for the embryo. An **embryo** is a tiny plant that will grow into a bigger plant.

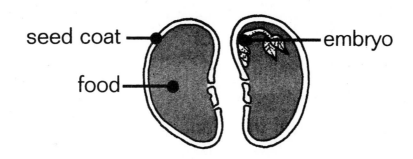

seed coat   embryo

food

Draw four seeds of different shapes and sizes. Write what kind of seed each one is.

1.	2.
_____	_____
3.	4.
_____	_____

From Seed to Plant

Most seeds can **sprout** without soil. But to grow into plants, seeds need soil, water, air, and warmth from the Sun. When they get what they need, plants can grow quickly.

In each box, draw one thing a seed needs to grow. Write on the line what it needs.

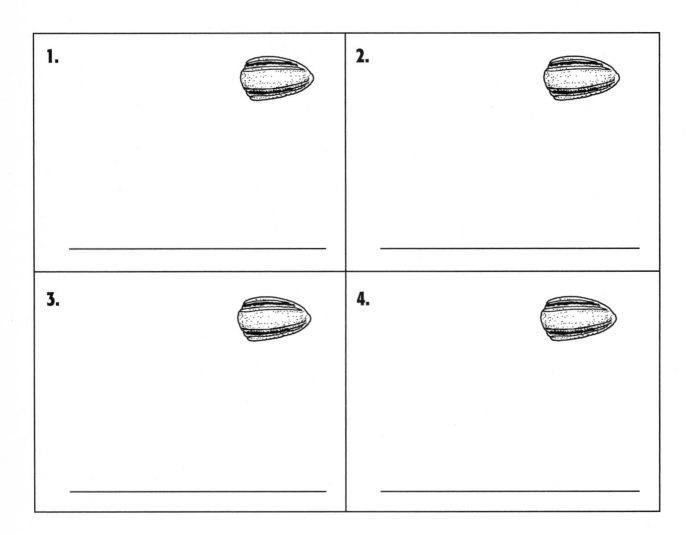

A growing plant can be very strong. A plant can push aside things that are in its way as it grows. A plant can move soil, gravel, and even rocks while it is growing.

In What Weather Do Seeds Grow Best?

Do seeds like warm weather? Or do they like cold weather? Do this activity to find out.

You will need
- ★ 2 dishes
- ★ 4 towels
- ★ seeds
- ★ refrigerator
- ★ water

1. Put a wet towel in each of two dishes.

2. Put some seeds on the towels.

3. Cover the seeds with another wet towel.

4. Put one dish in a warm place. Put the other dish in a cool place, like the refrigerator.

5. Check the seeds every day. Keep the towels moist.

Answer the questions.

1. Which seeds grew faster?

_____

_____

_____

2. Tell what weather is best for growing seeds.

_____

_____

_____

What Is in Soil?

There are little holes in the **soil** underground. The holes are filled with air. The air spaces give a plant's roots room to grow.

There is another reason for the holes underground. When it rains, the holes fill with water. The water mixes with **nutrients** in the soil. Then, the roots of plants take the water and the nutrients from the soil into the plants.

Draw a picture of how you think the soil looks underground.

Do Plants Need Sunlight and Air?

You know that plants need water to grow. But do they need sunlight and air? Find out in this activity.

aluminum foil

You will need
- ☆ potted plant
- ☆ aluminum foil
- ☆ plastic bag
- ☆ twist tie
- ☆ paper clip

1. Cover a leaf on a plant with aluminum foil. It will not get sunlight.

2. Cover another leaf with a plastic bag. This leaf will not get air.

3. Write down what you think will happen to each leaf.

4. Wait a week. Uncover the leaves.

📦 Answer the questions.

1. How does each leaf look now?

_____

_____

2. Do plants need air? Tell why you think so.

_____

_____

3. Do plants need sunlight? Tell why you think so.

_____

_____

What Kind of Soil Is Best for Plants?

There are many kinds of soil. What kind of soil is best for plants? Try this activity to find out. You will plant some bean seeds three ways.

You will need
- ★ sand
- ★ soil
- ★ 3 cups, paper or plastic
- ★ bean seeds

1. Put only sand in one cup. Label it **Cup A**.

2. Put only soil in one cup. Label it **Cup B**.

3. Put sand and soil in one cup. Label it **Cup C**.

4. Then, plant seeds in each cup. Put the cups near a window. Water them when needed.

5. Which seeds grow best? Keep a record in the chart.

	Date seeds came up	Date beans had 2 leaves	Date beans had 3 leaves
SAND Cup A			
SOIL Cup B			
SAND AND SOIL Cup C			

What Happens to Plants in the Cold?

Do plants like very cold weather? Try this activity to find out.

You will need
- ☆ 2 small stems from a houseplant
- ☆ 2 small stems from an evergreen tree
- ☆ 2 plastic or paper cups
- ☆ water

1. Put water in the cups.

2. Put one of each stem in the cups.

3. Put one cup in the freezer. Leave the other cup in the room.

⬛ Answer the questions.

1. Look at the stems the next day. What happened?

_____

_____

2. Could houseplants live outside in freezing weather?

_____

_____

3. Could evergreen trees live outside in freezing weather?

_____

_____

Trees Go Through Changes

Trees change as the **seasons** change.

🔲 **Read to find out how a maple tree changes. Then, color the pictures to show how a maple tree looks in each season.**

spring

The air becomes warmer. Buds open. Little leaves begin to grow on the tree.

summer

The air grows warmer still. Big, green leaves now cover all the branches of the tree.

fall

The air cools off. The leaves on the tree turn yellow and red. They begin to fall.

winter

This is the coldest season. The tree's branches are bare or covered with snowflakes.

Plant Game

 Answer the questions to move forward.

Winner

18.
Name four things a plant needs to grow.

Free Space

19.
Name a leaf we eat.

20.
What part of the plant makes seeds?

21.
Name a plant that can survive in a desert.

17.
Name one way seeds are spread from place to place.

16.
What part of a plant is the trunk of a tree?

15.
Name a root we eat.

14.
Name one thing that is inside a seed.

13.
What kind of leaves do evergreen trees have?

Free Space

Free Space

9.
Name a stem we eat.

Free Space

10.
Name three things a plant needs.

11.
Name one way earthworms help plants.

12.
There is one kind of root, true or false?

8.
What part of the plant makes food for the rest of the plant?

7.
What two things do roots do for a plant?

6.
Name two things a plant needs to live.

Free Space

5.
Name a fruit we eat.

4.
Name two things a stem does for a plant.

1.
Name one thing a plant needs to live.

Free Space

2.
Where do roots usually grow?

3.
Name a nut we eat.

Free Space

Start

Mammals Are Animals

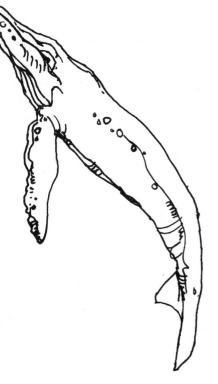

Mammals are animals that are covered with hair. Mammals are alike in other ways. A mammal grows inside its mother's body. Then, it is born. A young mammal drinks milk from its mother's body.

Most mammals move about on two or four legs. But whales are mammals, even though they don't have legs. Whales have a tiny bit of hair on their smooth skin. A whale is born, and it drinks milk from its mother's body.

Which words tell about a mammal? Write <u>yes</u> or <u>no</u>.

_____ **1.** has feathers

_____ **2.** has hair on its body

_____ **3.** is born live

_____ **4.** drinks milk from its mother's body

Mammals Crossword

Complete the puzzle.

Down

1. Mammals have _____ that covers their skin.

3. All mammals are born _____ .

4. Mammals drink _____ from their mothers.

Across

2. Mammals are _____ -blooded animals.

5. Mammals breathe with their _____ .

6. Mammals take care of their _____ .

Some Animals Live in Water

These are all animals that live in water. Three of these animals are **fish**. One of them is not a fish. How can you tell?

Like other living things, fish need air. Fish get the air they need from water. Fish have **gills**. Water flows through the fish's gills. Then, air passes out of the water and into the gills. Blood carries air from the gills to all parts of the fish's body.

Which animal is not a fish? The dolphin. It is a mammal. The dolphin breathes air through its mouth.

 Color the fish in the picture.

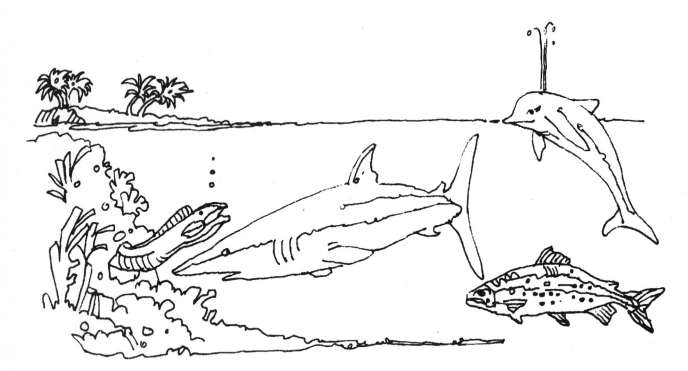

Go Fish!

How much do you know about fish? Complete this page to find out.

 Label the parts of a fish.

a. _____

b. _____

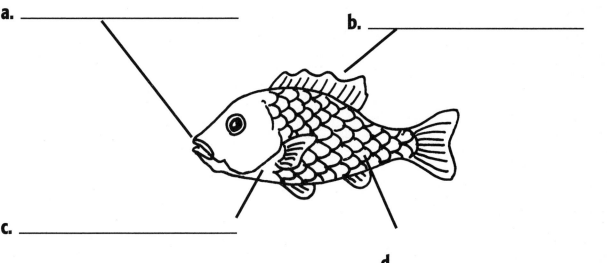

c. _____

d. _____

 Draw a line to match the term with its meaning.

Scales	• help the fish move.
Gills	• helps the fish eat.
Fins	• help protect the fish.
Mouth	• help the fish breathe.

 List some fish that you know.

1. _____

2. _____

3. _____

4. _____

Birds of a Feather

These animals are **birds**. They are alike in several ways. They all have feathers, and they all have wings. Birds hatch from eggs. They also have two legs.

Birds can be many sizes, shapes, and colors. Hummingbirds are some of the smallest birds. One kind of hummingbird is no bigger than your finger. The ostrich is the biggest bird. It can be taller than the tallest person.

 **Color the pictures of the birds. Color their feathers to show that birds can look different from one another.**

Feed the Birds!

Birds eat many kinds of food. Some birds eat insects. Others eat fish. Some birds eat fruits, and others eat seeds.

Here are some things some children left in a bird feeder for birds to eat. They put them in the feeder in the morning.

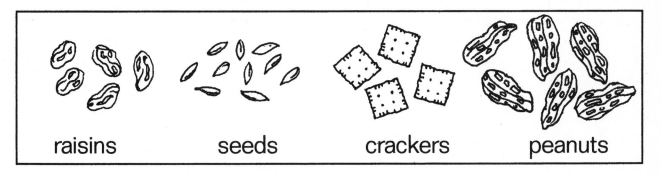

raisins   seeds   crackers   peanuts

Here is what was left in the feeder in the afternoon.

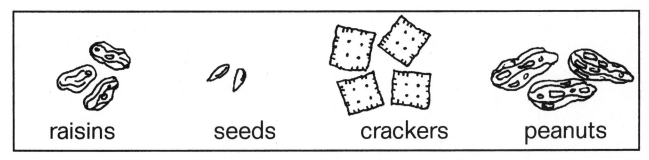

raisins   seeds   crackers   peanuts

1. How many of each food did the birds eat?

The birds ate _____ raisins, _____ seeds,

_____ crackers, and _____ peanuts.

2. Which food did the birds like best?

_____

_____

Why Are a Bird's Feathers Important?

A bird's body is covered with **feathers**. What are the feathers for? Do this activity to find out.

You will need
☆ feathers ☆ straw or eyedropper ☆ water

1. Collect some feathers.

2. Look at the feathers. Feel them.

3. Put a drop of water on each one.

Answer the questions.

1. Tell what happened to the water on each feather.

_____

_____

2. Do you think birds get wet when it rains? Why?

_____

_____

3. What are other ways that feathers are important to a bird?

_____

_____

Reptiles

Reptiles are animals that have a body covered with **scales**. The turtle has scales that fit together like pieces of a puzzle. They look like this.

Snakes have scales that do not fit together like puzzle pieces. Instead, they cover over each other. By themselves, the scales look like this.

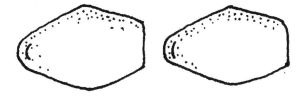

On the snake, the scales look like this.

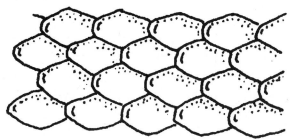

🔲 **These reptiles are missing their scales. Draw them in.**

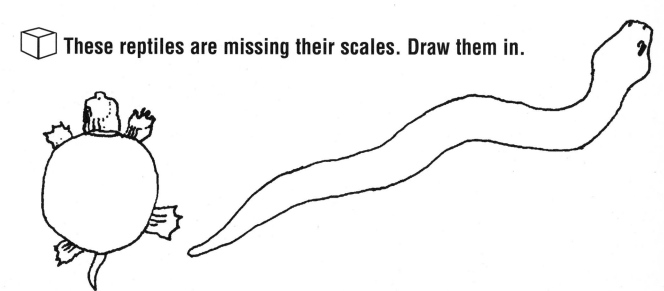

Snake!

Snakes have no legs. How do they move about? Snakes move by crawling. Some snakes crawl forward. Other snakes, like the sidewinder, crawl sideways.

Snakes have **fangs**, but they have no teeth. How do they eat? Snakes use their fangs to catch their food. Then, they swallow their food whole.

Snakes are covered with scales. What does a snake's skin feel like when you touch it? It feels dry. It does not feel slimy.

 Answer <u>yes</u> or <u>no</u>.

1. Do snakes chew their food? _____

2 Do all snakes crawl forward? _____

3. Is a snake's skin slimy? _____

 Draw and color your own picture of a snake.

Name _____ Date _____

Amazing Amphibians

Amphibians are animals that are born in the water and grow to live on the land. They have smooth, wet skin. Amphibians are cold-blooded animals. They use the Sun for energy. Amphibian babies grow from eggs, which are laid in water. As they grow, they undergo a great change. This is called **metamorphosis**. They grow from eggs to tadpoles with gills and tails. They can breathe in the water. Then, they grow legs and lungs. When their tails and gills disappear, they leave the water to live on land.

Most amphibians have legs and webbed feet. When amphibians are young, they eat only plants. When they are older, most amphibians become meat-eaters. Frogs, toads, and salamanders are all amphibians.

Darken the letter by the answer that best completes each sentence.

1. Amphibians have _____ skin.
   Ⓐ smooth   Ⓑ scaly   Ⓒ dry

2. Amphibians live _____.
   Ⓐ on land   Ⓑ in water   Ⓒ on land and in water

3. Adult amphibians eat _____.
   Ⓐ plants   Ⓑ meat   Ⓒ plants and meat

4. What are four stages of an amphibian as it grows? Write your answer.

   _____

   _____

   _____

   _____

   _____

Every Insect!

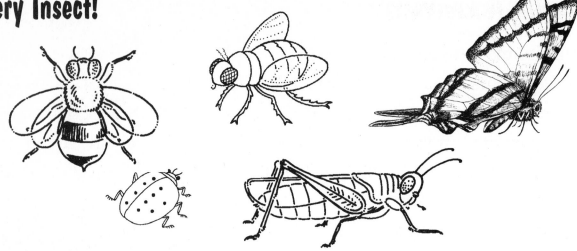

These animals are **insects**. They are alike in several ways. They all have six legs. They all have three body parts. They have two feelers. Insects have no bones inside their bodies. Instead, they have a skeleton on the outside of their bodies.

Answer the questions

1. How many body parts does an insect have?_____

2. How many legs does an insect have?_____

3. How many feelers does an insect have?_____

Draw and color a picture of an insect.

Insects Are Everywhere

There are more insects than all other animals put together! Why do you think this is true? Insects can multiply quickly. One insect can lay hundreds of eggs. Insects eat many different things. Sometimes they cause problems. Farmers must protect their crops against insects.

 **Take a walk near your home. Look for signs of insects.**

Can you find leaves that were eaten or chewed? Can you find fruit that has holes? Look under old bark and under rocks. Make a list of everything you find.

_____   _____

_____   _____

_____   _____

_____   _____

_____   _____

_____   _____

_____   _____

Animal Chart

Fill in the chart about each animal. Use books to help you.

Animal	What animal group does it belong to?	Where does the animal live?	Is the animal warm-blooded?	How is it born?	What is its skin covering like?

Endangered Animals

Giant pandas are **endangered** animals. That means they are in danger of becoming **extinct**. There are only about 1,000 of them left. They live in the mountain forests of China. If they become extinct, no pandas will be left.

Pandas are plant eaters. Their favorite food is bamboo. They eat from 22 to 44 pounds (10 to 20 kilograms) of bamboo every day. It takes them about 14 hours a day just to eat!

People used to hunt pandas for their fur. Now, there are laws against this. But pandas are still in danger because they can't find enough bamboo to eat. Many of the bamboo forests have been cut down to make way for houses and fields.

People are trying to help keep pandas alive. They have made special parks where pandas can come to get extra bamboo.

 **Draw and color a habitat for this giant panda.**

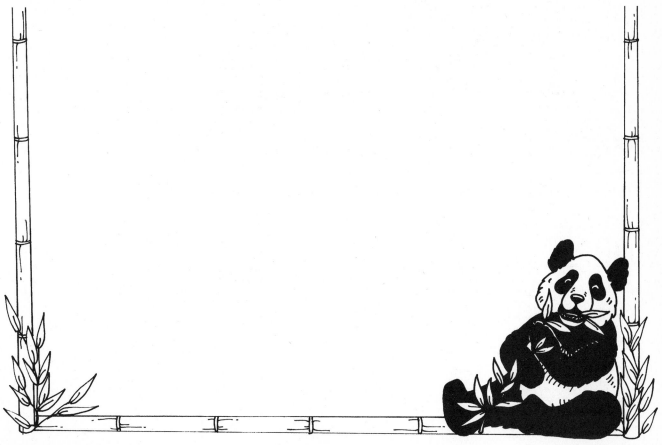

How Can We Save the Animals?

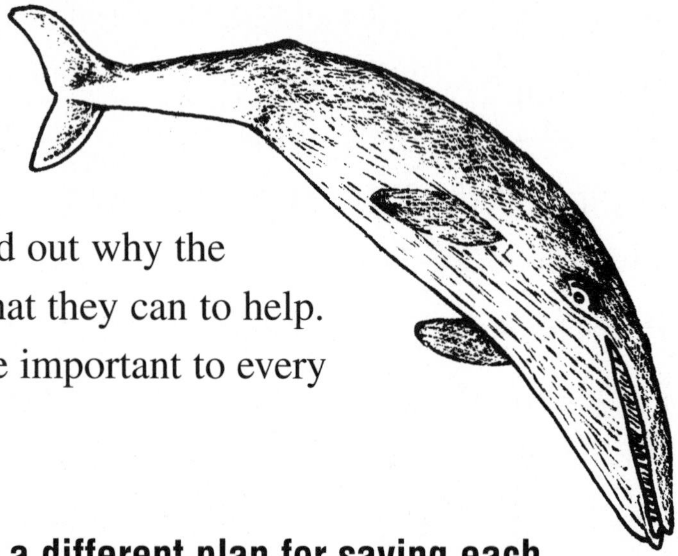

Many people all over the world
are trying to save endangered
animals. To do this, people have to
make a plan. The plan is different
for each kind of animal. People find out why the
animal is in trouble and then do what they can to help.
They know that all living things are important to every
other living thing on our planet.

Why do people need to make a different plan for saving each different kind of endangered animal? Write your answer.

_____

_____

_____

_____

_____

_____

_____

Eating Well

To be healthy, you need many different foods. Do you eat the right number of servings from each group?

 **Color the foods in each group.**

Vegetables and Fruits

Eat four servings each day.

Bread and Cereal

Eat four servings each day.

Meat and Beans

Eat two servings each day.

Milk

Eat two servings each day.

What Do You Eat in One Day?

📦 **Carry this chart with you for one day. Write down what you eat.**

	Vegetable-Fruit Group	Bread-Cereal Group	Meat-Bean Group	Milk Group
Breakfast				
Lunch				
Dinner				
Snacks				

Staying Healthy

Do you know the things you need to do to stay healthy?

 Look at the pictures. Complete each sentence.

1. W_____ every day.

2. Brush your t_____.

3. Eat good f_____.

4. Go to b_____ early.

Our Five Senses

We learn about the world by using our five **senses**. We see, hear, smell, taste, and touch things.

 How do we learn about these things? Draw lines to show.

1. 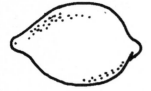   see

2.    hear

3.    smell

4.    taste

5.    touch

My Sense Observation

 Complete each sentence.

This morning, I tasted _____

_____

_____

On my way to school, I saw _____

_____

_____

In school, I heard _____

_____

_____

After school, I smelled _____

_____

_____

At bedtime, I felt _____

_____

_____

Your Heart and Lungs

Your **heart** and **lungs** are important **organs**. Do you know where they are?

Do this activity to find out.

You will need

★ a long roll of paper about 24 inches (60 cm) wide
★ colored markers

1. From the roll of paper, cut a piece long enough to lie down on.

2. Have a friend trace your body on the paper.

3. Draw in your heart. It is about the size of your fist.

4. Draw in your lungs. Each lung is about the size of your open hand.

5. Draw in your sense organs, too!

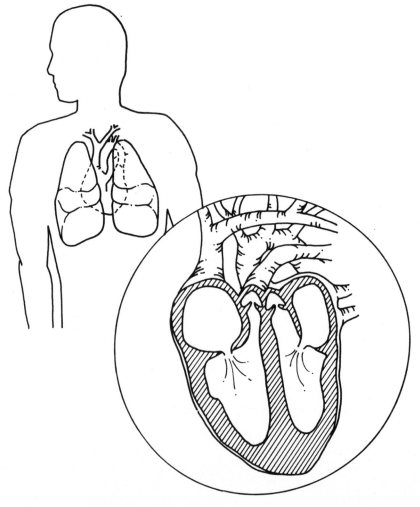

A Checkup

You should go to the doctor often for a **checkup**. Do you know what the doctor does in a checkup?

 Draw lines from the sentences to the correct pictures.

1. The doctor checks your ears.

A

2. The doctor measures your height and weight.

B

3. The doctor looks at your throat.

C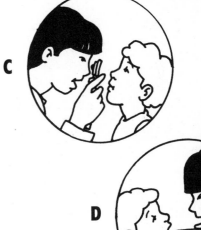

4. The doctor checks your eyes.

D

5. The doctor listens to your heart.

E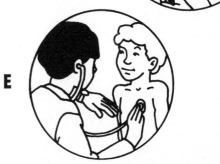

Do You Take Good Care of Yourself?

Do you take good care of yourself? Take this test to find out.

📦 **Check Yes or No for each question.**

	Yes	No
1. I eat many different kinds of foods.		
2. I get enough sleep every night.		
3. I wash my hands before I eat.		
4. I brush my teeth every morning and night.		
5. I visit the dentist at least once a year.		
6. I run around and play each day.		
7. I don't eat a lot of candy and other sweets.		
8. I wear warm clothes when it is cold outside.		

Did you answer <u>Yes</u> to every question? If so, then you do take good care of yourself.

📦 **Draw a picture of yourself doing one of the healthy things above.**

Water Safety Rules

Do you know how to be safe in the water?

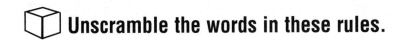 **Unscramble the words in these rules.**

1. __ __ __ __ __ how to swim.
E R L N A

2. Always __ __ __ __ with someone.
M I W S

3. Swim only where a lifeguard is __ __ __ __ __ __ __ .
T C I A W G H N

4. Never call for __ __ __ __ unless you really need it.
E P H L

5. Swim only in water that is __ __ __ __ for swimming.
A F S E

6. When boating, always wear a __ __ __ __ jacket.
F I E L

7. Do not __ __ __ __ into water if you do not know the depth.
I D V E

Bicycle Safety Rules

Follow these rules when you ride your bicycle.

1. Ride on the right-hand side of the street.

2. Obey all traffic signs.

3. Use hand signals.

4. Have a light on your bicycle if you ride at night.

5. Wear light-colored clothing.

6. Always wear a helmet.

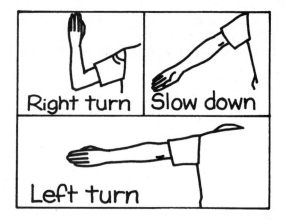

Right turn   Slow down   Left turn

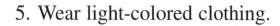 **Are these children following bicycle safety rules? Circle those who are. Put an X on those who are not.**

Science Grade 2 Answer Key

Pages 4–6
1. liquid, **2.** force, **3.** heavy, **4.** see, **5.** Sun, **6.** straight, **7.** soft, **8.** throats, **9.** true, **10.** false, **11.** true, **12.** true, **13.** C, **14.** A, **15.** B, **16.** B, **17.** habitat, **18.** roots, **19.** leaves, **20.** Seeds, **21.** soil, **22.** mammals, **23.** safe, **24.** bicycle

Pages 13–14
1. false, **2.** true, **3.** false, **4.** true, **5.** true; **6.–8.** Answers may vary.; **6.** shape, **7.** speed, **8.** direction, **9.** gas, **10.** bright, **11.** reflects, **12.** light, **13.** blocks, **14.** Sounds, **15.** high, **16.** air

Page 15
Answers will vary.

Page 16
1. S, **2.** G, **3.** S, **4.** L, **5.** G, **6.** L, **7.** L, **8.** S, **9.** G

Page 17
1. soccer ball, **2.** trash can, **3.** party hat, **4.** ice cube

Page 18
1. solid, **2.** gas, **3.** liquid

Page 19
Possible answer: Air takes the shape of its container, and it is invisible.

Page 20
1. left side, **2.** right side, **3.** right side, **4.** left side

Page 21
Answers will vary.

Page 22
The mass of the frozen water is the same as the mass of liquid water.

Page 23
1. yes, **2.** no, **3.** yes, **4.** yes

Page 24
Drawings will vary., no

Page 25
1. Students draw lettuce, celery, carrots, tomatoes., **2.** Students draw apples, oranges, grapes., **3.** Children draw two socks and a shirt.

Page 26
Let the water evaporate, and the sugar would be left.

Page 27
1. Answers will vary., **2.** Answers will vary from 32°F (0°C) to 40°F (4°C)., **3.** Answers will vary from 75°F (24°C) to 100°F (38°C).

Page 28
Check students' work.

Page 29
1. The heat will change the batter into pancakes.; circle, **2.** The heat will change the ice into water.; do not circle, **3.** The heat will change the dough into bread.; circle

Page 30
1. pull; Arrow points toward girl., **2.** pull; Arrow points in direction boy is moving., **3.** push; Arrow points away from boy., **4.** push; Arrow points away from girl., **5.** push; Arrow points down., **6.** push; Arrow points down.

Page 31
1. The clay became thinner and bigger in shape., **2.** The clay became thinner and longer in shape., **3.** Pushing and pulling are forces that change the shape of clay.

Page 32
Students circle the lawn mower and airplane and color the horse.

Page 34
1.–2. Answers will vary. Students should note that more washers are needed to move the object up the ramp., **3.** It is easier to walk down a hill., **4.** More force is needed to move an object up a hill.

Page 35
1.–2. Answers will vary., **3.** You would need more force because heavier things need more force to move them.

Page 37
oil—smooth; powder—smooth; sand—rough, **1.** Oil and powder are easier., **2.** Oil and powder make things move more easily., **3.** Possible answer: when moving a heavy box

Page 38
Answers may vary. **1.** hard, **2.** easy, **3.** hard, **4.** easy, **5.** hard

Page 39
1. sandpaper, carpet, sidewalk, **2.** tile, gym floor, **3.** Rough surfaces slow down things., **4.** Answers will vary. Possible answer: A rough surface that keeps people from slipping down or that slows sliding things would be good.

Page 40
Possible answers: roller skates, bicycles, cars, trucks, trains, vacuums, lawn mowers

Page 41
1. person, **2.** raindrops, **3.** person, **4.** apple

Page 42
1. 40, **2.** Students color Ei.

Page 43
Students circle the candle, Sun, flashlight, firefly, bulb, television. Students draw an X on the window, tree, stop sign. Students color the Sun, flashlight, bulb, and television yellow. Students color the candle and firefly blue.

Page 44
1. Nothing could be seen in the box with the lid closed because there was no light., **2.** The crayon could be seen when the lid was lifted because light entered the box., **3.** Light is needed for your eyes to see.

Page 46
1. Answers will vary. Some possible answers include clear cellophane or glass., **2.** Answers will vary. Some possible answers include foil, paper, corduroy., **3.** It is helpful to have light while reading, working, or playing.

Page 48
1. Yes, **2.** No, **3.** Light moves in straight lines, and the corner blocked the light. The mirror changed the direction of the light because it reflected the light around the corner., **4.** A periscope is a device to look around corners. It uses mirrors to change the direction of light two times.

Page 49

1. The mirror was the best reflector., 2. The surface of the mirror was smooth, flat, and shiny., 3. A good reflector has a smooth, shiny surface., 4. Light from cars hits the smooth, shiny surface of the bicycle reflector. It bounces back to the light source.

Page 51

1.–2. Answers will vary., 3. Yes; The shadow was thinner and more narrow in the morning., 4. The different position of the Sun made the shadow change.

Page 53

1. red, orange, yellow, green, blue, indigo (bluish purple), violet (purple), 2. The prism changed the direction of the light and bent it., 3. No; All light is made the same. The colors will be the same in the same order.

Page 54

1. The ruler moved up and down., 2. The sound was louder., 3. The sound became lower., 4. Sounds are made by vibrations. The faster the vibrations, the louder the sound. The more the ruler hung off the table, the slower the vibrations and the lower the sound.

Page 55

1. The sound changed when the pencil moved or when the rubber band was snapped hard or gently., 2. A sound is loud if the rubber band is plucked hard and soft if it is plucked gently., 3. A high sound can be made by shortening the part of the rubber band that vibrates. A low sound can be made by lengthening the part that vibrates.

Page 56

1. The sound was louder when using the bag filled with air., 2. Sounds travel better through air than cotton., 3. Possible answers: thick wood, Styrofoam, concrete

Page 57

1. low, 2. medium, 3. high

Page 58

1. The throat makes vibrations., 2. The vibrations become stronger when the humming gets louder., 3. Answers will vary., 4. The air coming from the lungs makes the vocal cords vibrate.

Page 59

Step 2: high, Step 3: low; Students circle the second guitar.

Page 60

Answers will vary. Possible answers: rugs, posters, banners, mobiles

Page 61

1. Answers will vary, but students should be able to point in the right direction most of the time., 2. Answers will vary, but students should have fewer correct answers., 3. People can hear better with two ears, because both ears catch sound waves as they move through the air.

Pages 69–70

1. false, 2. true, 3. true, 4. false, 5. false, 6. false, 7. true, 8. false, 9. false, 10. false, 11. C, 12. B, 13. C, 14. B, 15. A, 16. A, 17. B, 18. B, 19. C, 20. B

Page 71

1. B, 2. C; Students should color all land green and all water blue.

Page 72

1. a. crust, b. mantle, c. core, 2. Both have three layers. The egg has a thin shell, a thicker white, and a yolk at the center., 3. Both have three layers. The apple has a thin outer skin or peel, a thick part in the middle, and a core at the center.

Page 73

1. granite, 2. limestone or chalk, 3. lava or pumice, 4. pumice, 5. coal

Page 74

1.–2. Answers will vary. Have students describe how they grouped the rocks., 3. Rocks can be grouped by color, size, shape, and texture.

Page 75

Answers will vary.

Page 76

1. Drawing should show a smoother, smaller rock., 2. Drawing should show a smoother, smaller rock.

Page 77

1. Drawing should show an object before it has been eroded by water., 2. Drawing should show the same object after it has been eroded by water.

Page 78

Students' drawings should show a landform, such as a mountain, valley, plain, delta, plateau, butte, canyon, or cave, that was formed by the movement of wind or water.

Page 79

1. top picture, 2. bottom picture

Page 80

Answers will vary.

Page 81

1. Potting soil has bits of peat moss that comes from dead plants. Sand has bits of rock in it. Soil from outside may have clay, dead plant matter, insect parts, and rock in it., 2. The soils are different in color and texture. Potting soil has the finest texture. Outside soil may clump together if it contains a lot of clay.

Page 82

Students should draw and color some fossils in the bottom rock layer.

Page 83

Students should color fossils in the bottom layer. Possible answer: The oldest rock layer is on the bottom, so the fossils in that layer are the oldest, too.

Page 84

Possible answer: Two different kinds of dinosaurs walked next to each other, so they must have lived during the same period.

Page 85

Accept all colors.

Page 86

Possible answer: I think dinosaurs died out because the weather changed.

Page 87

1. Sun, 2. cloud, 3. evaporate, 4. rain, 5. ocean

Page 88

Students should draw an arrow in 9 places: steam from kettle, water in sponge, water in fishbowl, water from faucet, water from wet dish towel, water from wet dishes in drainer, water from houseplant, water from wet mop and puddle, water from bucket.

Page 90

1. Yes, **2.** No; The level changed more in the areas of the room that were warmer., **3.** The water evaporated., **4.** Answers may vary. The water evaporated and became water vapor in the air.

Page 91

1. water droplets, **2.** clear, **3.** no, **4.** The drops would be colored if they came from inside the can.

Page 92

1. The towel was wet., **2.** The towel was drier., **3.** The heat and the wind helped dry the towel that was outside.

Page 93

1. Air escaped from the glass and formed bubbles., **2.** The air moved because water rushed in to fill the glass when it was tilted. The water pushed the air out of the glass., **3.** Yes, air takes up space. It kept the water from going into the bottom of the glass before it was tilted.

Page 94

1. It became smaller than the other balloon and caused its end of the stick to rise., **2.** The side with the balloon full of air is heavier. It is heavier because air has weight.

Page 95

Under the rainy picture: It is a wet day. The wind is blowing. The air feels cool. Under the sunny picture: It is a dry day. It is not windy. The air feels warm.

Page 96

Answers will vary.

Page 98

1.–2. Answers will vary depending on the types of clouds seen and the weather., **3.** The clouds' shape and color help us know if the weather will be fair, rainy, or snowy. (Large, thick clouds mean thunderstorms; dark, layered, streaked clouds mean rain or snow; thin, high, feathery clouds mean fair weather; thick dome-shaped clouds mean fair weather.)

Page 99

1. cotton balls, **2.** good weather, **3.** dark rain clouds, **4.** rainy weather; Pictures: The top four show good weather; the bottom four show rainy weather.

Page 100

1. clouds, **2.** rain, **3.** wind, **4.** lightning, **5.** snow, **6.** Sun

Page 102

1–2. Answers will vary., **3.** Students may say they used today's weather to help predict tomorrow's weather. Or they may say they listened to a forecaster on TV or radio.

Page 103

1. snowy picture, **2.** rainy picture, **3.** sunny picture, **4.** windy picture

Page 104

Stories will vary but should include some of the thunderstorm safety rules.

Page 105

Possible answer: Shadows move because the Earth rotates once each day.

Page 106

Students should draw the shadows in the direction away from the Sun.

Page 107

Students should color the top, the boat, and the plane.

Page 108

Students' three drawings should show a shadow that changes in size and position as the Sun moves.

Page 111

2. Mercury, **3.** Venus, **4.** Earth, **5.** Mars, **6.** Jupiter, **7.** Saturn, **8.** Uranus, **9.** Neptune, **10.** Pluto

Page 112

1. Earth, Mars, and Jupiter, **2.** Mars, **3.** Earth, **4.** Jupiter, **5.** Earth, **6.** Earth and Mars, **7.** Earth and Mars, **8.** Jupiter, **9.** Jupiter, **10.** Earth, **11.** Mars

Page 113

Answers will vary.

Page 114

Students should color the sides of the Moon and the Earth farthest away from the Sun brown. They should color the sides closest to the Sun yellow.

Page 115

1. rotate, **2.** revolves, **3.** light, **4.** Sun, **5.** planets

Page 116

1. Big Dipper, **2.** Leo, **3.** Cassiopeia, **4.** Little Dipper, **5.** Orion

Pages 123–124

1. desert, **2.** rain forest, **3.** food, shelter, air, water, **4.** It destroys, or harms, them., **5.–8.** Students draw a flower showing the roots, stem, leaves, and blossoms. They label the leaves *a*, the stem *b*, the roots *c*, and the flower's blossom *d*.; Chart: Chart answers given left to right for each row: Mammal/has fur, soft/walks/live babies/hamster; Reptile/hard, dry scales/slithers/lays eggs/lizard; Amphibian/smooth, wet skin/hops or crawls/eggs in water/frog; Fish/has scales/swims/eggs in water/salmon; Bird/feathers/flies/eggs in nests/robin; Insect/hard body, 3 parts, or exoskeleton/crawls/eggs/ant; **9.–13.** Answers may vary., **9.** d, **10.** a, **11.** b, **12.** e, **13.** c

Page 125

Students should draw a line from the squirrel to the woods, from the seal to the ocean, from the kangaroo rat to the desert, and from the monkey to the rain forest.

Page 126

In any order: **1.** food, **2.** water, **3.** air, **4.** shelter

Page 127

Students draw worms in the tunnels; should show dead plants that they are eating.

Page 128

Students color all three cacti.

Page 129

Students circle the plant, the soil, and/or the Sun. Written answers will vary: Heat from the Sun causes the soil, the air, and the plant to release moisture.

Page 130

Drawings will vary.

Page 131

Check students' drawings for a sea creature that cannot live in fresh water, such as a shark, whale, shrimp, lobster, etc.

Page 132

Check students' drawings for correct labeling of roots, stems, and leaves.

Page 133

1. The potato grew small roots. The inside of the potato turned reddish in color., **2.** The potato changed because it was placed in water. It grew roots that absorbed some of the water.

Page 134

1. The leaves turned a reddish color., **2.** The tiny tubes of the stalk had red water in them., **3.** Water travels up through the stem to the leaves of a plant.

Page 135

taproot: long, thick; fibrous roots: short, thin

Page 136

Students draw arrows from the tips of the roots up to the blossom of the plant and to the leaves.

Page 137

Students' drawings will vary.

Page 138

Students should draw the Sun and water and/or air.

Page 139

Students' drawings will vary.

Page 140

In any order, students should draw soil, water, air, and Sun.

Page 141

1. The seeds in the warm place grew faster., **2.** Warm weather is best for seeds to grow. This is why seeds sprout and grow in the spring and not in the winter.

Page 142

Drawings will vary.

Page 143

1. Both leaves are limp and yellowish-brown., **2.** Plants need air. The leaf that was covered with a plastic bag did not receive air and is not healthy., **3.** Plants need sunlight. The leaf that was covered with foil did not receive sunlight and is not healthy.

Page 144

Dates will vary.

Page 145

1. The houseplant's leaves are frozen and wilted. The evergreen leaves are alive., **2.** No, **3.** Yes

Page 146

Check students' work.

Page 147

1. & 6. water, air, sunlight, **2.** in the soil, **3.** Possible answer: pecan, **4.** Carries water and nutrients to the leaves and flowers; holds the plant up to the Sun, **5.** apples, **7.** Carry water and nutrients; hold the plant in the ground, **8.** the leaves, **9.** Possible answer: celery, **10. & 18.** water, air, sunlight, soil (nutrients), **11.** They dig tunnels that bring water and air to the roots., **12.** false, **13.** needle leaves, **14.** Possible answer: the embryo, **15.** Possible answer: carrots, **16.** the stem, **17.** Animals carry seeds on their fur., **19.** Possible answer: lettuce, **20.** the flowers, **21.** a cactus

Page 148

1. no, **2.** yes, **3.** yes, **4.** yes

Page 149

DOWN: **1.** fur, **3.** alive, **4.** milk; ACROSS: **2.** warm, **5.** lungs, **6.** babies

Page 150

Students should color all animals but the dolphin.

Page 151

a. mouth, **b.** fin, **c.** gills, **d.** scales; Scales help protect the fish., Gills help the fish breathe., Fins help the fish move., Mouth helps the fish eat.; **1.–4.** Answers will vary.

Page 152

Check students' work.

Page 153

1. The birds ate 2 raisins, 8 seeds, 0 crackers, and 3 peanuts., **2.** seeds

Page 154

1. The water rolled off the feathers instead of soaking into the feathers., **2.** Birds do not get wet when it rains because the oil in their feathers sheds water so the rain never reaches the bird's body., **3.** Feathers help birds to stay warm; feathers form a smooth surface that reduces air friction and helps birds to fly; tail feathers help birds to steer in flight.

Page 155

Check students' work.

Page 156

1. no, **2.** no, **3.** no

Page 157

1. A, **2.** C, **3.** B, **4.** egg, tadpole with gills, tadpole with legs and lungs, adult

Page 158

1. 3, **2.** 6, **3.** 2

Page 159

Check students' work.

Page 160

Dog: mammal, on land, warm-blooded, alive, fur; Bird: bird, on land, warm-blooded, hatches from eggs, feathers; Fish: fish, in water, cold-blooded, from eggs, scales; Frog: amphibian, near water, cold-blooded, from eggs, smooth; Snake: reptile, on land, cold-blooded, from eggs or alive, scales

Page 161

Drawings will vary.

Page 162

Answers will vary. A different plan is needed for each animal because each animal has a different type of problem.

Page 164

Check students' charts.

Page 165

1. Wash, **2.** teeth, **3.** foods, **4.** bed

Page 166

Answers may vary. **1.** lemon/taste, **2.** cactus/touch, **3.** television/see, **4.** rose/smell, **5.** radio/hear

Page 167

Students' observations will vary. Introduce this exercise to students early in the day. Discuss the kinds of things they should think about writing as they go through the day. Have students complete the exercise at home and bring it back to school for the next day's class.

Page 168

Check students' drawings.

Page 169

1. B, **2.** A, **3.** D, **4.** C, **5.** E

Page 170

Check students' work.

Page 171

1. Learn, **2.** swim, **3.** watching, **4.** help, **5.** safe, **6.** life, **7.** dive

Page 172

Students should circle the girl who is signaling and the boy who has his lights on. They should put an X on the girl who is running a red (stop) traffic light and the boy who is riding in traffic.